Discovering Computers
Student Success Guide

Discovering Computers
Student Success Guide

Gary B. Shelly

Misty E. Vermaat

Contributing Authors
Susan L. Sebok
Steven M. Freund

Australia • Canada • Denmark • Japan • Mexico • New Zealand • Philippines • Puerto Rico • Singapore • South Africa • Spain • United Kingdom • United States

COURSE TECHNOLOGY
CENGAGE Learning

Discovering Computers: Student Success Guide
Gary B. Shelly, Misty E. Vermaat

Vice President, Career & Consulting: David Garza

Executive Editor: Kathleen McMahon

Associate Acquisitions Editor: Reed Curry

Associate Product Manager: Caitlin Womersley

Editorial Assistant: Sarah Ryan

Director of Marketing: Elisa Roberts

Senior Marketing Manager: Tristen Kendall

Marketing Coordinator: Michael Saver

Print Buyer: Julio Esperas

Content Project Manager: Matthew Hutchinson

Development Editor: Lyn Markowicz

Management Services: PreMediaGlobal

Interior Designer: Joel Sadagursky

Art Director: Jackie Bates

Text Design: Joel Sadagursky

Cover Design: Curio Press

Cover Photos: Tom Kates Photography

Illustrator: PreMediaGlobal

Compositor: PreMediaGlobal

Printer: RRD Jefferson City

For product information and technology assistance, contact us at
Cengage Learning Customer & Sales Support, 1-800-354-9706

For permission to use material from this text or product, submit all requests online at **cengage.com/permissions**
Further permissions questions can be emailed to
permissionrequest@cengage.com

Library of Congress Control Number: 2012930421

ISBN-13: 978-1-133-59345-4

ISBN-10: 1-133-59345-3

Course Technology
20 Channel Center Street
Boston, MA 02210
USA

Cengage Learning is a leading provider of customized learning solutions with office locations around the globe, including Singapore, the United Kingdom, Australia, Mexico, Brazil, and Japan. Locate your local office at:
international.cengage.com/region

Cengage Learning products are represented in Canada by Nelson Education, Ltd.

Visit our website www.cengage.com/ct/shellycashman to share and gain ideas on our textbooks!

To learn more about Course Technology,
visit **www.cengage.com/coursetechnology**

Purchase any of our products at your local college store or at our preferred online store **www.CengageBrain.com**

Printed in the United States of America
2 3 4 5 6 18 17 16 15 14 13 12

Every student can be successful in classes utilizing *Discovering Computers*. Establishing goals for what students want to achieve in the course and knowing how to best use the tools available in the textbook and in the Computer Concepts CourseMate will help every student succeed in this course.

This Student Success Guide can help students succeed in this course in the following ways:

Perform better on tests and quizzes

This guide points to content and resources in the textbook and in the Computer Concepts CourseMate to assist with learning key terms, studying important concepts, and reviewing essential material. The Chapter Study Guide focuses on the most important material in each chapter and challenges students to complete questions in the Study Guide, helping reinforce the concepts learned.

Enable retention of material and promote transference of knowledge

Each chapter is organized into several different general goals students might have for the course, like being an informed digital consumer, and categorizes the content and resources available in the textbook and in the Computer Concepts CourseMate to help students achieve those goals. The Chapter Study Guide in each chapter helps solidify and confirm that students understand the material presented.

Understand the relevance of this material

Computing and technology is everywhere. Learn about why this material matters in everyday life with the scenarios and thought-provoking questions at the beginning of each chapter that relate chapter content and resources to students' day-to-day life.

Keep current with technology

This guide presents ways for students to learn about the latest advances, changes, trends, breakthroughs, and products associated with computers, devices, and related technologies. Search phrases enable students to explore independently for information online.

Learn how to most effectively use the Computer Concepts CourseMate and WebTutor content

A comprehensive user guide demystifies the wealth of learning tools available on the Computer Concepts CourseMate and enables students to take advantage of all the Computer Concepts CourseMate has to offer learners. The WebTutor user guide will help students to best utilize the additional study tools available on WebTutor to maximize the learning experience.

New Learning Opportunities

New to the Computer Concepts CourseMate for *Discovering Computers* are three Web applications that can help student comprehension of the material when students are away from a computer. The Web applications available only via the Computer Concepts CourseMate are developed for use on smart phones, as well as on tablets, laptops, and desktop computers.

Improve retention of the chapter terms with the Flashcard Web application. Study for an exam by reviewing the major points in each chapter with the Study Guide Web application or with the Practice Test Web application that provides multiple choice quizzing.

Computer Concepts CourseMate enriches the *Discovering Computers* learning experience. For more information about the Computer Concepts CourseMate see the Preface of the *Discovering Computers: Your Interactive Guide to the Digital World* textbook for a Computer Concepts CourseMate walkthrough to learn more about the resources available on the Computer Concepts CourseMate for *Discovering Computers*.

Like us on Facebook and follow us on Twitter

Facebook posts and Twitter tweets will enable students and instructors to keep up-to-date quickly and easily with relevant technology changes and events in the computing industry. Become part of the Shelly Cashman *Discovering Computers* community.

For Instructors   A brand new testbank of questions for this edition of *Discovering Computers* promotes problem-solving and critical thinking, rather than requiring students merely to memorize and repeat the content in each chapter. Questions that challenge students to *think* about answers before responding ultimately creates a more solid, meaningful exam and assessment of student understanding of the material. All questions in the testbank relate to the Chapter Study Guide in the Student Success Guide.

Table of Contents

Discovering Computers
Student Success Guide
Chapters

Chapter 1

Student Success Guide

Introduction to Computers

Why Should I Learn About Computers?

"I use computers to do homework, search the Internet, check e-mail, play games, post updates on Facebook, talk on Skype, upload photos from my digital camera, sync music with my phone, and so much more! So, why am I in this class? What could I possibly learn?"

True, you may be familiar with some of the material in this chapter, but do you know . . .

"Why am I in this class?"

- How to protect yourself from identity theft? (p. 13, Ethics & Issues)
- Which game system you might use in physical therapy? (p. 24, Innovative Computing)
- What types of embedded computers you use every day? (p. 26, Embedded Computers)
- What types of computerized equipment an airplane's pilot uses to transport you safely to a destination? (p. 39, Computer Usage @ Work)
- How a GPS knows where you are all the time? (p. 40, High-Tech Talk)
- Which computer company sold more than five million units of a single phone model during just one quarter? (p. 41, Companies on the Cutting Edge)
- How to create a blog? (pp. 50–51 and Computer Concepts CourseMate, Learn How To)
- What steps to perform on your computer to determine its speed, its processor, and the amount of RAM it contains? (Windows Exercises, Computer Concepts CourseMate)

For these answers and to discover much more information essential to this course, read Chapter 1 and visit the associated Computer Concepts CourseMate at www.cengagebrain.com.

Customize Your Learning Experience

Q & A

How can I meet one or more of these goals?

Make use of the goal's resources for each chapter in the book and you should meet that goal by the end of the course.

Adapt this book to meet your needs by determining your goal. Would you like to be an informed digital consumer? A productive technology user? A safe user, protected from the risks in a digital world? A competent digital citizen? A future entrepreneur or professional in a digital society?

Every chapter in this Student Success Guide identifies resources targeted toward each of these goals, along with criteria to verify you understand the resources' content. Resources may be located in the textbook, on the Computer Concepts CourseMate Web site, in the interactive eBook, and on the Web.

Informed Digital Consumer

Goal: I would like to understand the terminology used in Web or print advertisements that sell computers, mobile devices, and related technology, as well as the jargon used by sales associates in computer or electronics stores, so that I can make informed purchasing decisions.

Topic	Resource	Location	Now you should . . .
Computer Hardware Components	Text/Figures	pp. 6–8	Know the purpose of input devices, output devices, the system unit, storage devices, and communications devices
	Drag and Drop Figure 1-3	eBook p. 7 or CourseMate	Be able to identify images on the Web or in magazines that show common computer hardware components
Types of Software	Text/Figures	pp. 15–16	Know the difference between system and application software
Personal Computers	Text/Figures	pp. 19–20	Know the difference between desktop and notebook computers
Mobile Devices	Text/Figures	pp. 20–23	Know the functions of tablets, smart phones, e-book readers, portable media players, and digital cameras
Camera Phones	Web Link	eBook p. 22 or CourseMate	Be able to identify the top camera phones and their features

Continued on next page

Continued from previous page

Topic	Resource	Location	Now you should . . .
Digital Cameras	Web Link	eBook p. 23 or CourseMate	Be able to identify the top point-and-shoot and SLR digital cameras, their features, and their current prices
Game Consoles	Text/Figure	p. 24	Know the types of game consoles
Apple	Text	p. 41	Be familiar with Apple's recent products and developments
	Link	eBook p. 41 or CourseMate	
Amazon	Text	p. 41	Be familiar with products and services available through Amazon
	Link	eBook p. 41 or CourseMate	
Learning About Your Computer	Windows Exercise	CourseMate	Know how to determine the processor type, speed, and amount of memory (RAM) on a Windows computer

Productive Technology User

Goal: I would like to learn ways that technology can benefit me at home, work, and school. I also would like to learn helpful techniques for using technology so that I can perform tasks more efficiently and be more productive in daily activities.

Topic	Resource	Location	Now you should . . .
Using the Internet	Text/Figures	pp. 11–14	Know why people use the Internet and the Web sites they use to share and interact with others
Most Visited Web Sites	FAQ Link	eBook p. 14, or Top Web Sites link, CourseMate	Know how to find widely used Web sites and how to determine any Web site's current ranking
Windows	Web Link	eBook p. 15 or CourseMate	Know how to access Microsoft's online tips and help for using Windows
	Labs	CourseMate	Be familiar with how to use the Windows interface
	Learn How To	p. 50 and CourseMate	Know how to start and close a program in Windows
Installing and Running Programs	Text/Figures and FAQ	pp. 16–17	Understand the processes of installing a program and running an installed program
	Drag and Drop Figure 1-12	eBook p. 17 or CourseMate	
Embedded Computers	Text/Figure	p. 26	Be familiar with everyday products that contain or could contain embedded computers
	Looking Ahead	p. 34	
	Link and Video	eBook p. 34 or CourseMate	
Home User	Text/Figure and FAQ	pp. 28–29	Know how technology can help home users
Mobile User	Text/Figure	p. 31	Know how technology can help mobile users
Education	Text/Figure	p. 34	Be able to identify ways people in education use computers
Finance	Text/Figure	pp. 34–35	Know how people use computers to assist with finances
Government	Text/Figure	p. 35	Be familiar with services offered online through government agencies
Travel	Text/Figure	p. 38	Know how people use computers in travel or with travel arrangements
	Web Link	eBook p. 38 or CourseMate	Know about OnStar and how to find vehicles with which it works
Using Input Devices	Labs	CourseMate	Know how to use a mouse and keyboard
Google Maps	Web Apps	CourseMate	Know how to use Google Maps to locate places and obtain directions

Safe User, Protected from the Risks in a Digital World

Goal: I would like to take measures to (1) protect my computers, devices, and data from loss, damage, or misuse; (2) minimize or prevent risks associated with using technology; and (3) minimize the environmental impact of using computers and related devices.

Topic	Resource	Location	Now you should . . .
Disadvantages of Using Computers	Text	pp. 9–10	Know the risks associated with using computers
Technology Overload	Ethics & Issues	p. 9	Recognize behaviors associated with technology overload
Green Computing	Text	p. 10	Know strategies that support green computing
	Web Link	eBook p. 10 or CourseMate	Know where to find the latest news related to green computing
Identify Theft and Phishing	Ethics & Issues	p. 13	Know the steps you can take to deter identity theft
	Video	eBook p. 13 or CourseMate	Describe ways to be safe from phishing attempts
Safety of Social Networking Web Sites	Ethics & Issues	p. 29	Know the types of problems that can arise from use of social networking Web sites
Privacy of Personal Information	Ethics & Issues	p. 35	Recognize the trade-offs associated with surrendering personal information
E-Waste	Ethics & Issues	p. 39	Know the potential hazards of e-waste and issues with recycling efforts

Competent Digital Citizen

Goal: I would like to be knowledgeable and well-informed about computers, mobile devices, and related technology, so that I am digitally literate in my personal and professional use of digital devices.

Topic	Resource	Location	Now you should . . .
Digital Literacy	Text	p. 5	Know why computer, or digital, literacy is vital to success
How Computers Process Data into Information	Text/Figure	p. 6	Be able to define the term, computer, and distinguish between data and information
	Figure 1-2 Animation	eBook p. 6 or CourseMate	Be able to identify examples of data, processes, and information
Advantages of Using Computers	Text	p. 9	Know the benefits of using computers
Google History	FAQ Video	eBook p. 14 or CourseMate	Be familiar with technological developments from Google
Computer and Video Games	FAQ Link	eBook p. 16, or Game Demographics link, CourseMate	Be familiar with demographics and statistics related to computer and video games and their players
Convergence	Text	p. 18	Be able to give examples of technological convergence
Categories of Computers	Drag and Drop Figure 1-14	eBook p. 19 or CourseMate	Be able to identify images on the Web or in magazines that show each category of computer
Users' Technology Requirements	Figure 1-35	p. 33	Be able to identify the hardware and software requirements for various types of users
Science	Text/Figure	pp. 36–37	Recognize how scientists' breakthroughs in technology assist society
	Figure 1-35 Video	eBook p. 37 or CourseMate	Understand the benefits of using camera pills for 3-D imaging

Continued on next page

Continued from previous page

Topic	Resource	Location	Now you should . . .
Determining Locations	Text/Figure	p. 40	Be familiar with how the Wii game console, GPS, and cell phones use triangulation to determine your location
	Link and Video	eBook p. 40 or CourseMate	
Bill Gates	Text	p. 41	Be familiar with Bill Gates impact on the personal computer and gaming industries and on society
	Link and Video	eBook p. 41 or CourseMate	
History of Computers and Other Digital Devices	Text/Figures	pp. 54–71	Be familiar with milestones in the history of computers and other digital devices
	Video	eBook p. 54 or CourseMate	
	Video	At the Movies, CourseMate	

Future Entrepreneur or Professional in a Digital Society

Goal: As I ponder my future, I envision myself as an entrepreneur or skilled professional using technology to support my business endeavors or job responsibilities. Along the way, I may interact with a variety of computer professionals — or I may just become one myself!

Topic	Resource	Location	Now you should . . .
Sharing Resources	Text	p. 10	Know why a business shares network resources
Software Development	Text	p. 18	Be able to identify the role of a computer programmer in a business
Apple vs. PC	FAQ Link	eBook p. 20, or Personal Computer Sales link, CourseMate	Be familiar with the types of personal computers being used in industry today
Handheld Computers	Text/Figure	pp. 22–23	Know how businesses use handheld computers
Servers, Mainframes, and Supercomputers	Text/Figures	p. 25	Know the purpose of servers, mainframes, and supercomputers, and their role in organizations
Information Systems	Text/Figure	p. 27	Understand how hardware, software, data, people, and procedures interact in an organization
	Drag and Drop Figure 1-29	eBook p. 27 or CourseMate	
SOHO User	Text/Figure	p. 30	Know how technology can help small office/home office users
Power User	Text/Figure	p. 31	Know how technology can help power users
Enterprise User	Text/Figure	p. 32	Know how technology can help an enterprise and its users
Health Care	Innovative Computing	p. 24	Understand how game consoles are used in the medical field to assist professionals and patients
	Link and Video	eBook p. 24 or CourseMate	
	Text/Figure	p. 36	Understand how technology assists medical professionals
Publishing	Text/Figure	p. 37	Understand how publishers use technology
Manufacturing	Text/Figure	p. 38	Understand how the manufacturing industry uses computers
Transportation	Computer Usage @ Work	p. 39	Know how professionals in the transportation industry use computers to support their activities
	Link and Video	eBook p. 39 or CourseMate	
Personal Computer Salesperson	Exploring Computer Careers	CourseMate	Be familiar with the responsibilities of and education required for a personal computer salesperson
Create and Use Your Own Blog	Learn How To	pp. 50–51 and CourseMate	Understand the benefits of blogs to business owners; know how to create a blog and format it for display on a mobile device

Preparing for a Test

Visit the Computer Concepts CourseMate at www.cengagebrain.com and then navigate to the Chapter 1 Web Apps resource for this book to prepare for your test.

Does your class use the Computer Concepts CourseMate Web site? If so, prepare for your test by using the Flash Cards, Study Guide, and Practice Test Web apps — available for your smart phone or tablet.

If your class does not use the Computer Concepts CourseMate Web site or you prefer to use your book, you can prepare for the test by doing the Quiz Yourself activities on pages 10, 18, and 38; reading the Chapter Review on pages 42–43; ensuring you know the definitions for the terms on page 44; and completing the Checkpoint exercises on pages 45–46. You also should know the material identified in the Chapter 1 Study Guide that follows.

Chapter 1 Study Guide

This study guide identifies material you should know for the Chapter 1 exam. You may want to write the answers in a notebook, enter them on your digital device, record them into a phone, or highlight them in your book. Choose whichever method helps you remember the best.

1. Define computer literacy, or digital literacy, and describe how its requirements change.

2. Define the term, computer.

3. Differentiate between data and information. Give an example of each.

4. Identify the activities in the information processing cycle.

5. Define the term, hardware. Give examples.

6. Describe the purpose of each of the five components of a computer: input devices, output devices, system unit, storage devices, and communications devices.

7. Identify examples of commonly used input devices, output devices, and storage devices.

8. The two main components on the motherboard are the _____ and _____.

9. List and describe five different advantages of using computers.

10. List and describe five different disadvantages of using computers.

11. Define the term, green computing. Describe strategies that support green computing.

12. Define the terms, network and online.

13. List two benefits of sharing resources on a network. Identify four types of resources that can be shared on a network.

14. Define the term, Internet. Identify reasons people use the Internet.

15. Differentiate between a Web page and a Web site.

16. Understand how phishing can lead to identity theft. Identify three ways to deter identity theft.

17. Explain the purpose of a social networking Web site. _____ is a popular social networking Web site.

18. Define the term, blog. _____ is a popular microblog.

19. Define the term, podcast.

20. Define the term, Web application. Give some examples of software available as Web applications.

21. Name three characteristics that classify a Web site as Web 2.0.

22. FAQ stands for _____.

23. Define the term, software, and then give a synonym for this term. Identify where you can obtain software.

24. Describe the characteristics of a graphical user interface.

25. Differentiate between system software and application software.

26. Microsoft's personal computer operating system is called _____. Apple's is called _____.

27. Distinguish between installing a program and running a program. Describe how to determine if software will run on a computer.

28. Define the term, programmer. A computer programmer may be called a _____. Name some programming languages.

29. Know the categories of computers. Explain the concept of convergence, with respect to technology.

30. List the components of a personal computer. Identify two popular architectures.

31. Differentiate between a desktop computer and a notebook computer. Notebook computers are also known as _____ computers.

32. Describe a digital tablet, or tablet computer.

33. Describe the purpose of these mobile devices: smart phone, PDA, e-book reader, handheld computer, portable media player, and digital camera.

34. Differentiate among a text message, picture message, and video message.

35. Describe the purpose of earbuds.

36. Distinguish between a standard game console and a handheld game console. Identify popular models of game consoles. Explain how the medical field uses the Wii game console.

37. Differentiate among a server, mainframe, and supercomputer.

38. Define the term, embedded computer. Give examples of products that contain embedded computers.

Continued on next page

Continued from previous page

39. Identify the five elements of an information system.

40. Explain the role of an IT department.

41. Name the five categories of users and describe how each uses technology.

42. Describe how technology is used in education, finance, government, health care, science, publishing, travel, manufacturing, and transportation.

43. Identify reasons e-waste can be hazardous and issues with recycling efforts.

44. Explain uses of triangulation and how a GPS determines a location.

45. Identify Apple's tablet, portable media player, smart phone, and its online music store.

46. Amazon's e-reader is called the _____.

47. Bill Gates founded _____.

48. Technology milestones: Who was Dr. Grace Hopper? Who built the first Apple computer? When did the IBM PC enter the personal computer marketplace? Who invented the World Wide Web? Which online company started as a bookstore? Which online social network was originally available only to college students? When did federal law require all full-power television stations broadcast only in digital format? What was the benefit of HTML5?

Check This Out

As technology changes, you must keep up with updates, new products, breakthroughs, and recent advances to remain digitally literate. The list below identifies topics related to this chapter that you should explore to keep current. In parentheses beside each topic, you will find a search term to help begin your research using a search engine, such as Google.

1. **popular Web applications** (search for: Web apps)

2. **widely used Web sites** (search for: best Web sites, or popular Web sites)

3. **latest version of the Windows operating system** (search for: Microsoft Windows versions)

4. **latest version of the Mac OS operating system** (search for: Apple Mac OS versions)

5. **latest version of the iPad and iPhone operating system** (search for: iOS version)

6. **latest version of the Android operating system** (search for: Android version)

7. **widely used apps for tablets** (search for: best tablet apps)

8. **widely used apps for smart phones** (search for: best phone apps)

9. **latest models of e-book readers** (search for: e-reader reviews)

10. **features of popular portable media players** (search for: portable media player features)

11. **widely used digital cameras** (search for: popular digital cameras)

12. **popular Xbox 360 games** (search for: top Xbox games)

13. **popular Wii games** (search for: top Wii games)

14. **popular PlayStation games** (search for: top PlayStation games)

15. **widely used travel Web sites** (search for: popular travel Web sites)

For current news and information
Check us out on Facebook and Twitter. See your instructor or the Computer Concepts CourseMate for specific information.

Student Success Guide
The Internet and the World Wide Web

Why Should I Learn About the Internet and the Web?

"I use the Internet and Web to shop for bargains, browse Google for all sorts of information, manage my fantasy sports teams, download music from iTunes, check e-mail on my phone, and so much more! Really, what more could I gain from the Internet or the Web?"

True, you may be familiar with some of the material in this chapter, but do you know . . .

"What more could I gain from the Internet or the Web?"

- Why you might support a do-not-track list? (p. 84, Ethics & Issues)
- Where you can obtain free plug-ins? (p. 97, Figure 2-24)
- How to create and publish your own Web page? (pp. 98 and 121 and Computer Concepts CourseMate, Learn How To)
- If you follow the code of acceptable behavior for online activities? (p. 108, Netiquette)
- How lighting technicians and audio engineers use computers to enhance your concert-going experiences? (p. 109, Computer Usage @ Work)
- How Mark Zuckerberg's college experiences led him to develop Facebook? (p. 111, Technology Trailblazers)
- How to search for a job online? (Student Edition Labs, Computer Concepts CourseMate)
- Which Web sites list job openings? (p. 138, Making Use of the Web Special Feature)

For these answers and to discover much more information essential to this course, read Chapter 2 and visit the associated Computer Concepts CourseMate at www.cengagebrain.com.

Customize Your Learning Experience

Q & A How can I meet one or more of these goals?

Make use of the goal's resources for each chapter in the book and you should meet that goal by the end of the course.

Adapt this book to meet your needs by determining your goal. Would you like to be an informed digital consumer? A productive technology user? A safe user, protected from the risks in a digital world? A competent digital citizen? A future entrepreneur or professional in a digital society?

Every chapter in this Student Success Guide identifies resources targeted toward each of these goals, along with criteria to verify you understand the resources' content. Resources may be located in the textbook, on the Computer Concepts CourseMate Web site, in the interactive eBook, and on the Web.

Informed Digital Consumer

Goal: I would like to understand the terminology used in Web or print advertisements that sell computers, mobile devices, and related technology, as well as the jargon used by sales associates in computer or electronics stores, so that I can make informed purchasing decisions.

Topic	Resource	Location	Now you should . . .
Broadband Internet Service and Providers	Text and FAQ	pp. 76–78	Know various high-speed alternatives for connecting to and accessing the Internet
	Labs	CourseMate	
Wireless Modems	Web Link	p. 78	Be able to identify various wireless modem options
Mobile Devices	FAQ Link	eBook p. 78, or Mobile Internet link, CourseMate	Be able to identify top mobile devices and accessories
iPhone	Web Link	p. 82	Know the features of the latest iPhone model
E-Commerce	Text	pp. 98–100	Know how to shop online or how an online auction works

Continued on next page

Continued from previous page

Topic	Resource	Location	Now you should . . .
Cartoon Animation Software	Video	eBook p. 109 or CourseMate	Be familiar with software that animates artwork
eBay	Text	p. 111	Be familiar with services offered by eBay
	Link	eBook p. 111 or CourseMate	

Productive Technology User

Goal: I would like to learn ways that technology can benefit me at home, work, and school. I also would like to learn helpful techniques for using technology so that I can perform tasks more efficiently and be more productive in daily activities.

Topic	Resource	Location	Now you should . . .
Internet Addresses	Text	pp. 79–80	Know the components of IP addresses and their relationship to domain names
Internet Connections	Labs	CourseMate	Know how to connect to and disconnect from the Internet
Internet Properties and Internet Explorer	Windows Exercises	CourseMate	Know how to modify Internet properties, including browsing history, security settings, and privacy controls; and how to use Internet Explorer
Web Browsing	Text	pp. 81–82	Be able to use and customize a Web browser
	Labs	CourseMate	
Web Addresses	Text	pp. 82–83	Know how to enter a Web address in a browser
	Drag and Drop Figure 2-8	eBook p. 83 or CourseMate	Know the components of a Web address (URL)
Navigating Web Pages	Text	pp. 83–84	Know how to use links to navigate Web pages
Tabbed Browsing	Web Link	eBook p. 84 or CourseMate	Be able to use tabbed browsing in Firefox
Searching the Web	Text and FAQ	pp. 85–88	Know how to use search engines and subject directories
	Drag and Drop Figure 2-11	p. 86	
	Drag and Drop Figure 2-13	p. 87	
	Labs	CourseMate	
	Learn How To	pp. 120–121 and CourseMate	
Evaluating a Web Site	Text	p. 92	Know the seven criteria for evaluating a Web site
	Drag and Drop Figure 2-16	eBook p. 92 or CourseMate	
WorldWide Telescope	Innovative Computing	p. 93	Know how to use a computer as a telescope
	Link	eBook p. 93 or CourseMate	
Downloading Music	Text	pp. 94–95	Know how to purchase, download, and listen to music
Web Video	Text and FAQ	p. 96	Know how to view video on a computer or device
	Web Link	eBook p. 96 or CourseMate	
	Figure 2-22 Video	eBook p. 96 or CourseMate	
Plug-Ins	Text	p. 97	Know the purpose of widely used plug-ins and where to download them

Continued on next page

Continued from previous page

Topic	Resource	Location	Now you should . . .
E-Mail	Text	pp. 101–103	Know various e-mail programs, and how to compose and send e-mail messages
	Figure 2-27 Animation	eBook p. 102 or CourseMate	
	Web Link	eBook p. 103 or CourseMate	
	FAQ	p. 105	
	Labs	CourseMate	
	Web Apps	CourseMate	
	Learn How To	p. 120 and CourseMate	
Instant Messaging	Text	pp. 104–105	Know how use instant messaging
Chat Rooms	Text	p. 105	Know how to use a chat room
VoIP	Text	p. 106	Know how VoIP works
Newsgroups	Text	p. 107	Be familiar with newsgroups
FTP	Text	p. 107	Know how to use FTP
	Web Link	eBook p. 107 or CourseMate	
Using Web Sites	Text	pp. 124–139	Be familiar with a variety of useful Web sites

Safe User, Protected from the Risks in a Digital World

Goal: I would like to take measures to (1) protect my computers, devices, and data from loss, damage, or misuse; (2) minimize or prevent risks associated with using technology; and (3) minimize the environmental impact of using computers and related devices.

Topic	Resource	Location	Now you should . . .
Web Site Tracking	Ethics & Issues	p. 84	Know the issues with Web site tracking and online profiles
Google Bombing	Ethics & Issues	p. 87	Recognize the effects of skewed search results
Using Wikis for Research	Ethics & Issues	p. 90	Describe the controversy surrounding using a wiki as a valid source of research
Shopping Online	FAQ	p. 99	Know safeguards when using credit cards online
	FAQ Video	eBook pg. 99 or CourseMate	
Online Payment Services	Text	p. 100	Be familiar with various online payment services designed to provide fraud protection
	Web Link	eBook p. 100 or CourseMate	
Communications	Ethics & Issues	p. 100	Be aware of how technology affects written and spoken words
E-Mail Viruses	FAQ	p. 103	Recognize that viruses can spread through infected e-mail attachments
Cyberbullying	Ethics & Issues	p. 108	Know how to identify cyberbullying and recognize ways to protect yourself from it
	Video	eBook p. 108 or CourseMate	
	Web Link	eBook p. 108 or CourseMate	

Competent Digital Citizen

Goal: I would like to be knowledgeable and well-informed about computers, mobile devices, and related technology, so that I am digitally literate in my personal and professional use of digital devices.

Topic	Resource	Location	Now you should . . .
Evolution of the Internet	Text	pp. 75–76	Know how the Internet evolved to its present day form
W3C	Text	p. 76	Know the role of W3C with the Internet and Web
	Web Link	eBook p. 76 or CourseMate	
Internet2	Text	p. 76	Know the goal of Internet2 and its projects
Internet Backbone	Text	pp. 78–79	Understand the basics of how data and information travel the Internet
	Drag and Drop Figure 2-3	eBook p. 79 or CourseMate	
Web and Web 2.0	Text	pp. 80–81	Recognize static and dynamic Web pages, and Web 2.0 sites
Web 3.0	Looking Ahead	p. 81	Understand the significance of Web 3.0
Web Site Types	Text	pp. 88–92	Know the purpose of various types of Web sites
Netiquette	Text	p. 108	Know the code of acceptable online behavior
Computers in Entertainment	Computer Usage @ Work	p. 109	Recognize how computers are used in music, movies, games, and performances
IP Addresses	Text	p. 110	Know the difference between an iPv4 and iPv6 address
	Video	eBook p. 110 or CourseMate	Know how to trace an IP address location
Google	Text	p. 111	Be familiar with Google's products and services
	Link	eBook p. 111 or Coursemate	
Tim Berners-Lee	Text	p. 111	Be familiar with the Internet and Web accomplishments and current endeavors of Tim Berners-Lee
	Link	eBook p. 111 or CourseMate	
Mark Zuckerberg	Text	p. 111	Be familiar with Mark Zuckerberg's impact on online social networks
	Link and Video	eBook p. 111 or CourseMate	

Future Entrepreneur or Professional in a Digital Society

Goal: As I ponder my future, I envision myself as an entrepreneur or skilled professional using technology to support my business endeavors or job responsibilities. Along the way, I may interact with a variety of computer professionals — or I may just become one myself!

Topic	Resource	Location	Now you should . . .
Popular Browsers	FAQ Link	eBook p. 82, or Browser Market Share link, CourseMate	Know the market share of browsers for desktop and mobile devices
Business/Marketing Web Sites	Text	p. 89	Know the purpose of a business Web site
RSS	Text	p. 92	Recognize the purpose of RSS and other feeds
Web Graphics Formats	Text	pp. 93–94	Know the available graphics formats for creating Web pages
Web Animation	Text	p. 94	Know ways that developers incorporate animation in Web pages

Continued on next page

Continued from previous page

Topic	Resource	Location	Now you should . . .
Web Audio - Formats and Distribution	Text	pp. 94–95	Know the available audio formats compatible with Web pages, and various methods of distributing audio on a Web page
Virtual Reality	Text	pp. 96–97	Know the reasons a business would use virtual reality
Web Publishing	Text	pp. 97–98	Know the steps to follow when developing and publishing a Web page
	Drag and Drop	p. 98	
	Learn How To	p. 121 and CourseMate	
Web Page Authoring	Web Link	eBook p. 98 or CourseMate	Know the tools developers use to create Web pages
Mailing Lists	Text	p. 103	Recognize why businesses use mailing lists
Video Blogs	Video	At the Movies, CourseMate	Know how to create and publish a video blog
Web Developer	Exploring Computer Careers	CourseMate	Be familiar with the responsibilities of and education required for a Web developer

Preparing for a Test

Visit the Computer Concepts CourseMate at www.cengagebrain.com and then navigate to the Chapter 2 Web Apps resource for this book to prepare for your test.

Does your class use the Computer Concepts CourseMate Web site? If so, prepare for your test by using the Flash Cards, Study Guide, and Practice Test Web apps — available for your smart phone or tablet.

If your class does not use the Computer Concepts CourseMate Web site or you prefer to use your book, you can prepare for the test by doing the Quiz Yourself activities on pages 80, 98, and 109; reading the Chapter Review on pages 112–113; ensuring you know the definitions for the terms on page 114; and completing the Checkpoint exercises on pages 115–116. You also should know the material identified in the Chapter 2 Study Guide that follows.

Chapter 2 Study Guide

This study guide identifies material you should know for the Chapter 2 exam. You may want to write the answers in a notebook, enter them on your digital device, record them into a phone, or highlight them in your book. Choose whichever method helps you remember the best.

1. List the two goals of ARPANET. Name the year it became functional.

2. Describe the role of a host on a network.

3. Explain how ARPANET, hosts, and NSFnet contributed to the evolution of the Internet.

4. Communications activity on a network is called _____.

5. Identify the role of the W3C.

6. Describe the goal of Internet2. Give some examples of its projects.

7. Briefly describe seven types of broadband Internet service.

8. State the purpose of a hot spot. Name locations you might find one.

9. Define the term, access provider.

10. Differentiate among a regional ISP, a national ISP, an online service provider, and a wireless Internet service provider.

11. Major carriers of Internet traffic are known collectively as the Internet _____.

12. Describe the purpose and composition of an IP address.

13. Define the term, domain name. Cite an example of one.

14. Know the purpose of several generic TLDs. Identify ICANN's role with TLDs.

15. State the purpose of a DNS server.

16. Differentiate between an IPv4 and IPv6 address. Discuss why IPv6 eventually will replace IPv4.

17. Distinguish among the Web, a Web page, a Web site, and a Web server. Describe the role of each when a browser displays a home page.

18. Explain the purpose of a Web browser. Name five popular browsers for personal computers.

19. A _____ is a built-in connection to another related Web page or part of a Web page.

Continued on next page

Continued from previous page

20. Define the terms, downloading and uploading.

21. Define the term, Web address. Name a synonym.

22. Name and give examples of the four components of a Web address. Identify the two components that may be optional.

23. State the purpose of a bookmark.

24. Describe what happens when you click a link.

25. Describe the function and purpose of tabbed browsing.

26. Differentiate between a search engine and a subject directory.

27. Besides Web pages, identify other types of items a search engine can find.

28. Describe how to use a search engine to search for information. Give an example of search text.

29. Relevancy and _____ are two criteria search engines use to determine the priority of search results. Describe ways to improve search results.

30. Know how and when to use these search engine operators: +, OR, ( ), -, " ", and *.

31. Describe the purpose of these types of Web sites: portal, news, informational, business/marketing, blog, wiki, online social network, educational, entertainment, advocacy, Web app, content aggregator, and personal.

32. Explain the controversy surrounding using a wiki as a valid source of research. Name a widely used wiki.

33. Describe seven criteria for evaluating a Web site's content.

34. Define the term, multimedia.

35. Explain how Web pages use graphics, animation, audio, video, virtual reality, and plug-ins.

36. Name the types of graphics formats used on the Web.

37. Define the term, thumbnail.

38. Name some popular audio file players.

39. Define the term, streaming. Identify uses of streaming audio.

40. Identify the purpose of popular plug-ins.

41. Identify and briefly describe the steps in Web publishing.

42. Define the term, e-commerce. Describe and give examples of the types of e-commerce: B2C, C2C, and B2B.

43. Describe the purpose of these Internet services and explain how each works: e-mail, mailing lists, instant messaging, chat rooms, VoIP, and FTP.

44. _____ and _____ are two popular free e-mail Web apps.

45. Describe the components of an e-mail address.

46. Define the term, real time.

47. Define the term, netiquette. Identify the rules of netiquette.

48. Describe cyberbullying, how it occurs, and why it is difficult to catch the perpetrators.

49. Describe the purpose of these Web sites: Google, Webopedia, Blogger, Bloglines, Twitter, Facebook, LinkedIn, flickr, Shutterfly, YouTube, Expedia, Maps.com, E*TRADE, THOMAS, craigslist, eBay, Amazon, The Weather Channel, Yahoo! Sports, MSNBC, HowStuffWorks, NASA, WebMD, Monster, and Project Gutenberg.

Check This Out

As technology changes, you must keep up with updates, new products, breakthroughs, and recent advances to remain digitally literate. The list below identifies topics related to this chapter that you should explore to keep current. In parentheses beside each topic, you will find a search term to help begin your research using a search engine, such as Google.

For current news and information
Check us out on Facebook and Twitter. See your instructor or the Computer Concepts CourseMate for specific information.

1. **standards that alert users to unauthorized Web tracking** (search for: W3C Web tracking alerts)

2. **broadband Internet service in rural areas** (search for: extend broadband rural)

3. **broadband upload and download speed tests** (search for: broadband speed test)

4. **new ICANN top-level domains** (search for: ICANN domain)

5. **popular mobile Internet Web sites** (search for: top mobile device sites)

6. **today's most common search queries** (search for: top search terms)

7. **widely used online social networks** (search for: online social networks)

8. **errors found in Wikipedia** (search for: Wikipedia mistakes)

9. **computer games and game player statistics** (search for: computer game industry statistics)

10. **latest Web graphics formats** (search for: latest Web image file types)

11. **latest version of iTunes** (search for: iTunes version)

12. **recent uses of virtual reality** (search for: virtual reality news)

13. **latest news about cyberbullying** (search for: cyberbullying laws)

14. **latest music apps** (search for: music apps)

15. **popular weather Web sites** (search for: weather sites)

Student Success Guide
Application Software

Why Should I Learn About Application Software?

"I use my computer mostly to type homework assignments, pay bills online, enhance digital photos, update my blog, and play games. Several years ago, a friend installed an antivirus program to protect my computer from viruses. What more software could I possibly need?"

True, you may be familiar with some of the material in this chapter, but do you know . . .

"What more software could I possibly need?"

- Which software can help you take notes? (p. 148, Figure 3-4, and p. 156)
- How teachers can detect Internet plagiarism in typed documents? (p. 149, Ethics & Issues)
- How fireworks shows use software to synchronize their displays with music? (p. 160, Innovative Computing)
- How CAD software helps architects and engineers design and construct buildings? (p. 160, Computer-Aided Design; p. 177, Computer Usage @ Work)
- How a computer virus unleashes its payload? (p. 178, High-Tech Talk)
- Which software company is the largest? (p. 179, Companies on the Cutting Edge)
- How to zip a file? (p. 189 and Computer Concepts CourseMate, Learn How To)
- How to use WordPad? (Windows Exercises, Computer Concepts CourseMate)
- Why texting can be harmful? (p. 196, Digital Communications Special Feature)

For these answers and to discover much more information essential to this course, read Chapter 3 and visit the associated Computer Concepts CourseMate at www.cengagebrain.com.

Q&A How can I meet one or more of these goals?

Make use of the goal's resources for each chapter in the book and you should meet that goal by the end of the course.

Customize Your Learning Experience

Adapt this book to meet your needs by determining your goal. Would you like to be an informed digital consumer? A productive technology user? A safe user, protected from the risks in a digital world? A competent digital citizen? A future entrepreneur or professional in a digital society?

Every chapter in this Student Success Guide identifies resources targeted toward each of these goals, along with criteria to verify you understand the resources' content. Resources may be located in the textbook, on the Computer Concepts CourseMate Web site, in the interactive eBook, and on the Web.

Informed Digital Consumer

Goal: I would like to understand the terminology used in Web or print advertisements that sell computers, mobile devices, and related technology, as well as the jargon used by sales associates in computer or electronics stores, so that I can make informed purchasing decisions.

Topic	Resource	Location	Now you should . . .
Software Availability	Text	pp. 142–143	Know the seven forms through which software is available
Registration	Text	p. 143	Be able to differentiate software registration from product activation
Business Software	Text/Figure	p. 146	Be able to identify widely used business programs
Business Software for Phones and PIM	Text/Figure	pp. 156–157	Know the types of business software available for phones and features of personal information manager software
Graphics and Multimedia	Text/Figure	pp. 159–160	Be able to identify widely used graphics and multimedia software
Graphics Software	Web Link	eBook p. 160 or CourseMate	Be able to identify the top graphics software and supporting devices

Continued on next page

Continued from previous page

Topic	Resource	Location	Now you should . . .
Home, Personal, Educational Software	Text/Figure	p. 165	Be able to identify widely used programs for home/personal/educational use
Tax Preparation	Link and Video	eBook p. 167 or CourseMate	Be able to identify the features of the top tax preparation programs
Adobe	Text	p. 179	Be familiar with Adobe's software
	Link	eBook p. 179 or CourseMate	
Microsoft	Text	p. 179	Be familiar with Microsoft's products and services
	Link and Video	eBook p. 179 or CourseMate	

Productive Technology User

Goal: I would like to learn ways that technology can benefit me at home, work, and school. I also would like to learn helpful techniques for using technology so that I can perform tasks more efficiently and be more productive in daily activities.

Topic	Resource	Location	Now you should . . .
Windows Programs	Text/Figure	pp. 144–145	Know Windows elements and how to start and use a program
	Drag and Drop Figure 3-3	p. 145	
Word Processing Software	Text/Figures	pp. 147–148	Know the features available in word processing software
	Web Link	eBook p. 148 or CourseMate	
	Ethics & Issues	p. 150	Know the issues surrounding word processing use
	Labs, Windows Exercises	CourseMate	Be able to use word processing software
Developing a Document	Text/Figure and FAQ	pp. 149–150	Understand the tasks involved with creating, editing, formatting, saving, and printing documents
	FAQ Link	eBook p. 150, or Saving Documents link, CourseMate	
	Windows Exercises	CourseMate	Know how to create a document in WordPad and use its Help feature
	Learn How To	eBook pp. 188–189 or CourseMate	Know how to save a file, install and uninstall a program, and zip a file
Spreadsheet Software	Text/Figures	pp. 150–153	Know the organization of and features in spreadsheet software
	Labs	CourseMate	Be able to use spreadsheet software
Database Software	Text/Figure and FAQ	pp. 153–154	Be able to describe a database, its organization, and how database software works
	Labs	CourseMate	Be able to use database software
Presentation Software	Text/Figures	pp. 154–155	Know the features available in presentation software
Note Taking Software	Text/Figure	p. 156	Know the function of note taking software
Business Software Suite	Text	p. 156	Know the programs in and advantages of a business software suite; give examples
	Web Link	eBook p. 156 or CourseMate	
Document Mgmt.	Text/Figure	p. 158	Know the purpose of document management software and PDF files

Continued on next page

Continued from previous page

Topic	Resource	Location	Now you should . . .
Personal Finance	Text/Figure and FAQ	p. 166	Know how to use personal finance software and online banking
Legal Software	Text/Figure	p. 167	Know the benefits of using legal software and types of documents provided
	FAQ Link	eBook p. 167, or Legal Software link, CourseMate	
Tax Preparation	Text/Figure	p. 167	Know the features of tax preparation software and benefits of e-filing
DTP Software	Text/Figure	pp. 167–168	Know the purpose of and how to use personal DTP software
	Web Link	eBook p. 168 or CourseMate	
Paint/Image/Photo Editing	Text/Figures	pp. 168–169	Know the purpose and capabilities of personal paint/image editing and photo editing software
	Figure Video	eBook p. 169 or CourseMate	
Clip Art/Image Gallery	Text/Figure	p. 169	Know the benefits of clip art/image gallery software
Video and Audio Editing	Text/Figure	p. 170	Know the basic features of video and audio editing software
	Video	At the Movies, CourseMate	Know how to convert media files to a format for mobile devices
Design/Landscaping	Text/Figure	p. 170	Know the basic features of home design/landscaping software
Travel and Mapping	Text/Figure	p. 170	Know the benefits of using travel and mapping software
Reference	Text/Figures	p. 171	Know various types of reference and educational software
Web Apps	Text/Figures	pp. 172–173	Know the purpose of several Web apps
	Web Link	eBook p. 173 or CourseMate	
	Web Apps	CourseMate	Know how to use Britannica.com
Communications	Text/Figure	p. 174	Know the purpose of a variety of programs used for home and business communications
	Drag and Drop Figure 3-44	eBook p. 174 or CourseMate	
Help	Text/Figure	p. 175	Understand how to use online and Web-based Help
iTunes U	Innovative Computing	p. 175	Know how to access lectures, demonstrations, and performances on iTunes U
	Link and Video		
Digital Communications – Personal Use	Text/Figures	pp. 194, 196, 198, 200, 202, and 204	Understand the advantages, disadvantages, and good practices in personal use of e-mail, text/picture/video messaging, blogs, wikis, online social networks, Web conferences, and content sharing

Safe User, Protected from the Risks in a Digital World

Goal: I would like to take measures to (1) protect my computers, devices, and data from loss, damage, or misuse; (2) minimize or prevent risks associated with using technology; and (3) minimize the environmental impact of using computers and related devices.

Topic	Resource	Location	Now you should . . .
Viruses and Antivirus Programs	Text & FAQ	p. 144	Know how computer viruses work, the role of an antivirus program, and how to protect a computer from viruses and other malware
	FAQ Link and Video	eBook p. 144, or Computer Viruses link, CourseMate	
	Web Link	eBook p. 144 or CourseMate	
	High-Tech Talk	p. 178	
	Link and Video		
Mapping Services	Ethics & Issues	p. 173	Be aware of issues surrounding mapping services

Competent Digital Citizen

Goal: I would like to be knowledgeable and well-informed about computers, mobile devices, and related technology, so that I am digitally literate in my personal and professional use of digital devices.

Topic	Resource	Location	Now you should . . .
Application Software	Text/Figure	p. 142	Be able to identify the primary use of various application software
System Software	Text/Figure	pp. 143–144	Know the role of system software with respect to application software
	Figure 3-2 Animation	eBook p. 143 or CourseMate	
Plagiarism	Ethics & Issues	p. 149	Know how teachers use software to detect plagiarism
Fireworks Software	Innovative Computing	p. 160	Understand how fireworks shows use software to coordinate music with the display
	Link	eBook p. 160 or CourseMate	
Digital Photo Alteration	Ethics & Issues	p. 162	Recognize how commercial or professional photos may be altered to a degree they are considered digital forgery
	Video	eBook p. 162 or CourseMate	
Driving Aids	Looking Ahead	p. 171	Be familiar with developments underway to assist drivers
	Link and Video	eBook p. 171 or CourseMate	
Entertainment	Text/Figure and FAQ	p. 172	Know examples of entertainment software
	Web Link	eBook p. 172 or CourseMate	
	FAQ Link	eBook p.172, or Entertainment Software link, CourseMate	
Distance Learning	Text/Figure	p. 176	Be familiar with the uses and benefits of DL training and education
Dan Bricklin	Text	p. 179	Be familiar with Dan Bricklin's contributions to the software industry
	Link	eBook p. 179 or CourseMate	

Future Entrepreneur or Professional in a Digital Society

Goal: As I ponder my future, I envision myself as an entrepreneur or skilled professional using technology to support my business endeavors or job responsibilities. Along the way, I may interact with a variety of computer professionals — or I may just become one myself!

Topic	Resource	Location	Now you should . . .
Database Options	Web Link	eBook p. 154 or CourseMate	Know the various database options for a business
Project Management	Text/Figure	p. 157	Know the purpose of project management software in business
Accounting Software	Text/Figure	p. 158	Know how companies use accounting software
Enterprise Computing	Text	p. 159	Know how functional business units use software
CAD	Text/Figure	p. 160	Know how engineers, architects, and scientists use CAD software
	Computer Usage @ Work	p. 177	
	Link and Video	eBook p. 177 or CourseMate	
DTP	Text/Figure	pp. 160–161	Know how professional designers use DTP software
Paint/Image Editing	Text/Figure	p. 161	Know how professionals use paint/image editing software
Photo Editing	Text/Figure	p. 162	Know how photo editing software assists professional photo users

Continued on next page

Continued from previous page

Topic	Resource	Location	Now you should . . .
Video and Audio Editing	Text/Figure	pp. 162–163	Know how professionals use video editing software and audio editing software
Multimedia Authoring	Text/Figure	pp. 162–163	Know how multimedia authoring software is used in business
Web Page Authoring	Text/Figure	p. 164	Know the purpose of Web page authoring software
	Web Link	eBook p. 164 or CourseMate	Be able to identify Web authoring tools and HTML editors
Help Desk Specialist	Exploring Computer Careers	CourseMate	Be familiar with the responsibilities of and education required for a help desk specialist
Digital Communications – Business Use	Text/Figures	pp. 195, 197, 199, 201, 203, and 205	Understand the advantages, disadvantages, and good practices in business use of e-mail, text/picture/video messaging, blogs, wikis, online social networks, Web conferences, and content sharing

Preparing for a Test

Visit the Computer Concepts CourseMate at www.cengagebrain.com and then navigate to the Chapter 3 Web Apps resource for this book to prepare for your test.

Does your class use the Computer Concepts CourseMate Web site? If so, prepare for your test by using the Flash Cards, Study Guide, and Practice Test Web apps — available for your smart phone or tablet.

If your class does not use the Computer Concepts CourseMate Web site or you prefer to use your book, you can prepare for the test by doing the Quiz Yourself activities on pages 146, 164, and 177; reading the Chapter Review on pages 180–181; ensuring you know the definitions for the terms on page 182; and completing the Checkpoint exercises on pages 183–184. You also should know the material identified in the Chapter 3 Study Guide that follows.

Chapter 3 Study Guide

This study guide identifies material you should know for the Chapter 3 exam. You may want to write the answers in a notebook, enter them on your digital device, record them into a phone, or highlight them in your book. Choose whichever method helps you remember the best.

1. Name four uses for application software.

2. Differentiate among packaged software, custom software, Web apps, open source software, shareware, freeware, and public-domain software.

3. Describe software registration and product activation.

4. Explain how the operating system and utility programs work with application software.

5. Name three popular personal computer operating systems.

6. Malicious software also is known as _____.

7. Identify ways a computer can be infected with a virus.

8. Describe common elements of the Windows user interface.

9. Explain the purpose of a file. Give an example of a file name.

10. Know how to start a Windows program.

11. Describe the features available in word processing software. Name popular word processing programs.

12. Explain the process of creating, editing, formatting, saving, and printing a document.

13. Differentiate between a serif font and a sans serif font.

14. Font size is gauged by a measurement system called _____.

15. Describe the features of spreadsheet software and the organization of a spreadsheet. Name popular spreadsheet programs.

16. Define the term, database. Describe how a database is organized and the purpose of database software. Name popular database programs.

17. Describe the features available in presentation software. Name popular presentation programs.

18. Identify the function and benefit of note taking software.

19. Identify programs typically in a business software suite and advantages of using a suite. Name popular business software suites.

20. Identify types of business software available for phones.

21. Describe the purpose and key features of project management software, accounting software, and document management software.

Continued on next page

Continued from previous page

22. Adobe Reader enables you to view any _____ file.

23. Briefly describe how functional business units in an enterprise use software.

24. Explain how engineers, architects, and scientists use CAD software.

25. Explain how professionals use DTP software, paint software, image editing software, photo editing software, video and editing software, and multimedia authoring software.

26. Identify the purpose and users of Web page authoring software.

27. Describe the benefits of personal finance software and online banking.

28. Identify the purpose of legal software.

29. Describe the purpose of tax preparation software. Define the term, e-filing.

30. Identify key features of these programs for personal use: desktop publishing, paint/image editing, photo editing, photo management, clip art/image gallery, video and audio editing, and home design/landscaping.

31. Describe features of travel and mapping software. Identify devices on which it usually is preinstalled.

32. Describe types of reference software and educational software.

33. Another word for computer-based training (CBT) is _____ (CAI). Identify some uses of CBT.

34. Describe types of entertainment software.

35. Define the term, cloud storage.

36. Describe the purpose of a Web app and various distribution methods. Name popular Web apps.

37. Identify issues surrounding online mapping services.

38. Describe the purpose of these application programs for communications: Web browser, e-mail, text/picture/video messaging, RSS aggregator, blogging, FTP, VoIP, and video conferencing.

39. Define the terms, online Help and Web-based Help.

40. Describe the purpose of iTunes U. Identify who posts its content.

41. Define the term, Web-based training.

42. Explain the advantages of distance learning.

43. Describe how instructors use e-learning providers to enhance their courses.

44. Briefly describe three actions a virus may perform during its infection phase.

45. Give examples of what might occur when a virus unleashes its payload.

46. Identify steps to protect a computer from virus infections.

47. Identify the names of Adobe's widely used programs.

48. Identify some of Microsoft's products and services.

49. Identify the advantages with personal and business use of e-mail, text/picture/video messaging, blogs, wikis, online social networks, Web conferences, and content sharing.

Check This Out

As technology changes, you must keep up with updates, new products, breakthroughs, and recent advances to remain digitally literate. The list below identifies topics related to this chapter that you should explore to keep current. In parentheses beside each topic, you will find a search term to help begin your research using a search engine, such as Google.

For current news and information
Check us out on Facebook and Twitter. See your instructor or the Computer Concepts CourseMate for specific information.

1. **widely used freeware** (search for: popular freeware)

2. **malware attacks on mobile devices** (search for: mobile malware)

3. **business letter writing tips** (search for: writing business letters)

4. **presentation software design principles** (search for: presentation software slide design)

5. **business software apps for smart phones** (search for: best business apps)

6. **latest version of Adobe Reader** (search for: Adobe Reader version)

7. **check deposit using a smart phone** (search for: remote deposit smart phone)

8. **popular photo editing software** (search for: best photo editing software)

9. **widely used computer games** (search for: top computer games)

10. **current productivity Web apps** (search for: productivity Web apps)

11. **new iTunes U course lectures** (search for: iTunes U lectures)

12. **recent computer viruses** (search for: latest computer viruses)

13. **latest Microsoft news** (search for: Microsoft news)

14. **latest news about online social networks** (search for: social network news)

15. **top blogs** (search for: best blogs)

Why Should I Learn About System Unit Components?

"I bought my computer a few years ago, and it appears to be working well. Although at times it seems to run a little slow and it generates a lot of heat, I have not had problems with it. So, why do I need to learn about hardware in the system unit?"

True, you may be familiar with some of the material in this chapter, but do you know . . .

- What types of processors can improve your computer's speed? (p. 213, Processor)
- How computer chips can help you locate a lost pet? (p. 213, Innovative Computing)
- How manufacturers name their processors? (p. 217, Comparison of Personal Computer Processors)
- Why the Department of Homeland Security may search your notebook computer at the airport? (p. 217, Ethics & Issues)
- How the sports industry uses computers? (p. 241, Computer Usage @ Work)
- Which company is the world's leading chip manufacturer? (p. 243, Companies on the Cutting Edge)
- How to purchase and install computer memory? (pp. 252–253 and Computer Concepts CourseMate, Learn How To)
- How to monitor your computer's electric consumption? (Windows Exercises, Computer Concepts CourseMate)

"Why do I need to learn about hardware in the system unit?"

For these answers and to discover much more information essential to this course, read Chapter 4 and visit the associated Computer Concepts CourseMate at www.cengagebrain.com.

Customize Your Learning Experience

Q & A How can I meet one or more of these goals?

Make use of the goal's resources for each chapter in the book and you should meet that goal by the end of the course.

Adapt this book to meet your needs by determining your goal. Would you like to be an informed digital consumer? A productive technology user? A safe user, protected from the risks in a digital world? A competent digital citizen? A future entrepreneur or professional in a digital society?

Every chapter in this Student Success Guide identifies resources targeted toward each of these goals, along with criteria to verify you understand the resources' content. Resources may be located in the textbook, on the Computer Concepts CourseMate Web site, in the interactive eBook, and on the Web.

Informed Digital Consumer

Goal: I would like to understand the terminology used in Web or print advertisements that sell computers, mobile devices, and related technology, as well as the jargon used by sales associates in computer or electronics stores, so that I can make informed purchasing decisions.

Topic	Resource	Location	Now you should . . .
ID Chips	Innovative Computing	p. 213	Know how ID chips help locate lost pets, along with other uses of the chips and approximate cost
	Link	eBook p. 213 or CourseMate	
Personal Computer Processors	Text/Figures	pp. 216–218	Know the popular chips by AMD and Intel, and their intended use
Chip Technology	Web Link	eBook p. 217 or CourseMate	Be familiar with current and future chip-making technologies
Cooling Kits	Web Link	eBook p. 220 or CourseMate	Know the features and approximate prices of computer cooling kits

Continued on next page

Continued from previous page

Topic	Resource	Location	Now you should . . .
Memory Sizes	Text/Figure	p. 223	Know the terms and acronyms used to define memory sizes
	Drag and Drop Figure 4-17	eBook p. 223 or CourseMate	
RAM Types and Requirements	Text/Figure	pp. 224–226	Know the types of RAM chips and guidelines for amount of RAM needed when purchasing or upgrading
	Drag and Drop Figure 4-19	eBook p. 225 or CourseMate	
	FAQ and Link	eBook p. 226 or CourseMate	
	Learn How To	pp. 252–253	
Cache	Text/Figure	p. 227	Know the types of cache and their capacities
Memory Access Times	Text/Figures	p. 229	Know the terms and acronyms used to define memory access times
	Drag and Drop Figure 4-24	eBook p. 229 or CourseMate	
Adapter Cards	Text/Figure	pp. 230–231	Know the purpose of widely used types of adapter cards
	Drag and Drop Figure 4-26	eBook p. 230 or CourseMate	
Video Cards, etc.	Web Link	eBook p. 230 or CourseMate	Be familiar with video cards and other components you can purchase
Removable Flash Memory	Text/Figure	p. 231	Be familiar with the purpose and use of memory cards, USB flash drives, and ExpressCard modules
Ports and Connectors	Text/Figures	pp. 232–236	Know the purpose of and be able to identify ports on desktop computers, notebook computers, and mobile devices
	Drag and Drop Figure 4-31	eBook p. 233 or CourseMate	
Processor and RAM	Figure 4-38	p. 239	Be familiar with processor and RAM recommendations for various users
NVIDIA	Text	p. 243	Be familiar with NVIDIA's products
	Link	eBook p. 243 or CourseMate	
Intel	Text	p. 243	Be familiar with Intel's products
	Link and Video	eBook p. 243 or CourseMate	

Productive Technology User

Goal: I would like to learn ways that technology can benefit me at home, work, and school. I also would like to learn helpful techniques for using technology so that I can perform tasks more efficiently and be more productive in daily activities.

Topic	Resource	Location	Now you should . . .
Windows ReadyBoost	Text	p. 227	Know how to use Windows ReadyBoost to increase a computer's memory
	Web Link	eBook p. 227 or CourseMate	
System Clock	Windows Exercises	CourseMate	Be able to set the system clock on a Windows computer
Flash Memory	Text/Figure	p. 228	Know examples of flash memory and how mobile devices use it

Continued on next page

Continued from previous page

Topic	Resource	Location	Now you should . . .
Portable Media Players	Figure and FAQ	pp. 228–229	Know how portable media players store music
	FAQ Link	eBook p. 229, or Portable Media Players link, CourseMate	
USB Ports	Text	p. 234	Know how to use a USB port
	Link and Video	eBook p. 234 or CourseMate	
FireWire	Text	p. 234	Know how FireWire works
	Web Link	eBook p. 238 or CourseMate	
Connecting Wireless Devices	FAQ	p. 235	Know how to connect wireless devices
	FAQ Link	eBook p. 235, or Wireless Devices link, CourseMate	
Installing Hardware	Windows Exercises	CourseMate	Be able to install a new device
Port Replicators and Docking Stations	Text/Figure	p. 236	Know the purpose of port replicators and docking stations, and their current prices
	Web Link	eBook p. 236 or CourseMate	
Bays	Text/Figure	p. 238	Know and be able to identify various types of bays
Power Supply and Fans	Text and FAQ	p. 239	Be familiar with the role of the power supply and types of computer fans and coolers
	FAQ Link	eBook p. 239, or Computer Fans link, CourseMate	
Apps for Sports Fans	Computer Usage @ Work	eBook p. 241 or CourseMate	Be familiar with phone and tablet apps for professional baseball and football
	Video		
Installing RAM	Video	eBook p. 242 or CourseMate	Know how to install RAM
	Learn How To	pp. 252–253	
Time Machine	Video	At the Movies, CourseMate	Know how to use Time Machine on an Apple computer to restore any previous files, data, or programs
Calculator	Labs and Windows Exercises	CourseMate	Know how to use Windows Calculator
Google Docs	Web Apps	CourseMate	Know how to use Google Docs to create documents, presentations, etc.

Safe User, Protected from the Risks in a Digital World

Goal: I would like to take measures to (1) protect my computers, devices, and data from loss, damage, or misuse; (2) minimize or prevent risks associated with using technology; and (3) minimize the environmental impact of using computers and related devices.

Topic	Resource	Location	Now you should . . .
Computer Search and Seizure	Ethics & Issues	p. 217	Be aware that the Dept. of Homeland Security can search and seize any mobile computer or device upon its arrival in the U.S.
Cleaning Computers and Mobile Devices	Text/Figure and FAQ	pp. 240–241	Know how to keep your computer and mobile device clean
Power Management	Windows Exercises	CourseMate	Be able to manage the power usage on your computer

Competent Digital Citizen

Goal: I would like to be knowledgeable and well-informed about computers, mobile devices, and related technology, so that I am digitally literate in my personal and professional use of digital devices.

Topic	Resource	Location	Now you should . . .
System Units	Text/Figures	pp. 210–212	Know the size and shape of system units on various computers and devices
Motherboard	Text/Figure	p. 212	Recognize the various slots, chips, and other items on a motherboard
	Labs	CourseMate	
System Unit Components	Drag and Drop Figure 4-3	p. 212	Be able to identify the items in and on a system unit
Processor	Text/Figures	pp. 213–215	Know the purpose of processors, relative speed of multi-core processors, and the role of the control unit and ALU
	Drag and Drop Figure 4-4	p. 213	
Robots	Innovative Computing	p. 214	Understand how robots assist with household and industrial tasks
	Link and Video	eBook p. 214 or CourseMate	
Turing Test	Ethics & Issues	p. 214	Be familiar with the Turing Test's relationship to computer intelligence
Machine Cycle	Text/Figures	pp. 215–216	Know the steps in a machine cycle and their relationship to processing speed
	Figure 4-5 Animation	p. 215	
Registers	Text	p. 216	Know the function of registers
System Clock	Text	p. 216	Know the purpose of the system clock and how clock speed is measured
Real-Time Clock	FAQ	p. 216	Know the difference between the system clock and the real-time clock
Processor Cooling	Text/Figures	pp. 219–220	Know the ways processor chips are cooled
Parallel Processing	Text/Figure	p. 220	Know the definition of parallel processing
Data Representation	Text/Figures	pp. 221–222	Understand how a computer represents data and uses coding schemes
	Labs	CourseMate	
Memory Storage	Text/Figure	p. 223	Know what items memory stores and how items are stored
Memory Types	Text	p. 223	Understand the difference between volatile and nonvolatile memory and types of RAM
	Link	eBook p. 242 or CourseMate	
RAM	Text/Figure	p. 224	Understand how program instructions transfer in and out of RAM
	Text/Figure	p. 242	Know the technical details about how RAM works
	Labs	CourseMate	
One Laptop per Child	Ethics & Issues	p. 226	Know the intent of the OLPC plan endorsed by the United Nations
	Video		See how the OLPCs work
ROM	Text	p. 228	Understand the purpose and types of ROM chips
	Labs	CourseMate	
CMOS	Text	p. 229	Be able to identify examples of CMOS use
Future Notebook Computers	Looking Ahead	p. 236	Know some of the current and future developments with respect to notebook computers
	Link and Video	eBook p. 236 or CourseMate	

Continued on next page

Continued from previous page

Topic	Resource	Location	Now you should . . .
Buses	Text/Figure	pp. 237–238	Know the parts of a bus, bus widths, and types of buses
Computers in Sports	Computer Usage @ Work	p. 241	Recognize how computers are used in professional baseball and NASCAR
	Link		
Jack Kilby	Text	p. 243	Be familiar with Jack Kilby's most significant patent
	Link	eBook p. 243 or CourseMate	
Gordon Moore	Text	p. 243	Be familiar with Moore's Law and other contributions from Gordon Moore
	Link	eBook p. 243 or CourseMate	

Future Entrepreneur or Professional in a Digital Society

Goal: As I ponder my future, I envision myself as an entrepreneur or skilled professional using technology to support my business endeavors or job responsibilities. Along the way, I may interact with a variety of computer professionals — or I may just become one myself!

Topic	Resource	Location	Now you should . . .
PC Market Share	FAQ	p. 219	Know the top PC vendors
Computer Factory	FAQ Video	eBook p. 219 or CourseMate	See how one PC vendor manufactures computers and fulfills orders
Computer Engineer	Exploring Computer Careers	CourseMate	Be familiar with the responsibilities of and education required for a computer engineer

Preparing for a Test

Visit the Computer Concepts CourseMate at www.cengagebrain.com and then navigate to the Chapter 4 Web Apps resource for this book to prepare for your test.

Does your class use the Computer Concepts CourseMate Web site? If so, prepare for your test by using the Flash Cards, Study Guide, and Practice Test Web apps — available for your smart phone or tablet.

If your class does not use the Computer Concepts CourseMate Web site or you prefer to use your book, you can prepare for the test by doing the Quiz Yourself activities on pages 220, 230, and 241; reading the Chapter Review on pages 244–245; ensuring you know the definitions for the terms on page 246; and completing the Checkpoint exercises on pages 247–248. You also should know the material identified in the Chapter 4 Study Guide that follows.

Chapter 4 Study Guide

This study guide identifies material you should know for the Chapter 4 exam. You may want to write the answers in a notebook, enter them on your digital device, record them into a phone, or highlight them in your book. Choose whichever method helps you remember the best.

1. Differentiate among the various styles of system units on desktop computers, notebook computers, and mobile devices.

2. Define the term, motherboard. Identify components that attach to the motherboard.

3. Define the term, computer chip.

4. Describe uses of chip implants.

5. A processor also is called a CPU, which stands for _____.

6. Describe the purpose of a processor. Describe multi-core processors.

7. Explain the role of the control unit and ALU in a computer.

8. Describe the purpose of the Turing Test.

9. Explain the four steps in a machine cycle.

10. Describe the benefit of pipelining.

11. Define the term, register. Identify functions of registers.

12. Identify the purpose of the system clock. Explain its relationship to the processor and devices.

13. One _____ (GHz) equals one billion ticks of the system clock per second.

14. Identify the clock that keeps track of the date and time in a computer and how it runs when the computer is off.

15. The leading manufacturers of personal computer processor chips are _____ and _____.

Continued on next page

Continued from previous page

16. Explain how processor manufacturers identify their chips.

17. Identify processor features unique to notebook computers and tablets.

18. Explain techniques used to dissipate processor heat.

19. Define the term, bit. The two digits used to represent bits are the _____ and _____.

20. Describe how a series of bits represents data.

21. Define the term, memory. Describe three types of items it stores.

22. Explain how memory uses addresses.

23. Differentiate among a kilobyte, megabyte, gigabyte, and terabyte. State their abbreviations.

24. Explain the difference between volatile and nonvolatile memory.

25. Explain how program instructions transfer in and out of memory.

26. Differentiate among DRAM, SRAM, and MRAM.

27. RAM chips usually reside on a _____ module.

28. Describe how to determine the amount of RAM necessary in a computer.

29. State the purpose of memory cache. Describe three types of memory cache.

30. Define the terms, ROM and firmware.

31. Define flash memory. Identify examples of its use.

32. Describe the advantage and uses of CMOS technology.

33. Define access time.

34. Differentiate among a millisecond, microsecond, nanosecond, and picosecond. State their abbreviations.

35. Describe the purpose of expansion slots and adapter cards.

36. Differentiate among a sound card, network card, and video card.

37. Define the term, Plug and Play.

38. Differentiate among a memory card, USB flash drive, PC Card, and ExpressCard module.

39. Explain the difference between a port and a connector.

40. Differentiate between a USB port and a FireWire port.

41. Explain the purpose of USB and FireWire hubs.

42. Briefly describe the purpose of a Bluetooth port, SCSI port, eSATA port, IrDA port, serial port, and MIDI port.

43. Explain the purpose of a port replicator and docking station.

44. Define the terms, bus and bus width.

45. Differentiate between the data bus and the address bus.

46. Describe the purpose of a front side bus, backside bus, and expansion buses.

47. Explain the purpose of a power supply.

48. Identify the various types of fans in a system unit.

49. Describe Moore's Law.

Check This Out

As technology changes, you must keep up with updates, new products, breakthroughs, and recent advances to remain digitally literate. The list below identifies topics related to this chapter that you should explore to keep current. In parentheses beside each topic, you will find a search term to help begin your research using a search engine, such as Google.

1. **latest tablet computers** (search for: tablets)

2. **recent uses of robotic technologies** (search for: new robot trends)

3. **fastest processor clock speeds** (search for: fastest processor)

4. **latest personal computer processors** (search for: processor comparison)

5. **top personal computer vendors** (search for: personal computer market share)

6. **new liquid cooling technology** (search for: liquid cooled computers)

7. **recent computer memory developments** (search for: new computer memory)

8. **One Laptop per Child notebook computers** (search for: OLPC stories)

9. **new removable flash memory devices** (search for: flash memory update)

10. **latest USB developments** (search for: USB news)

11. **latest Bluetooth technologies** (search for: Bluetooth improvements)

12. **docking stations for mobile devices** (search for: mobile device docking station)

13. **power supply heat problems** (search for: computer power supply heat)

14. **tablet computer use in professional sports** (search for: tablet professional sports)

15. **predictions based on Moore's Law** (search for: Moore's Law future)

For current news and information
Check us out on Facebook and Twitter. See your instructor or the Computer Concepts CourseMate for specific information.

Student Success Guide

Input

Why Should I Learn About Input Devices?

"After work or school, I video chat with my friends and discuss our gaming strategies. My computer has a wireless keyboard and mouse. I talk on a Bluetooth headset paired with my smart phone. I use my bank's ATM and the self-serve checkout at the grocery store. So, why do I need to learn about more input devices?"

True, you may be familiar with some of the material in this chapter, but do you know . . .

"Why do I need to learn about more input devices?"

- How your boss may monitor all the Web sites you visit while at work? (p. 261, Ethics & Issues)
- How to reduce the risk of injuring your wrists when you are typing? (p. 262, Keyboard Ergonomics)
- Which tabletop display Microsoft developed that has a touch screen and the ability to recognize fingers and objects? (p. 267, Touch Screens and Touch-Sensitive Pads)
- How a flatbed scanner converts a document into a digital image? (p. 278, Optical Scanners)
- How computers have increased accuracy and efficiency in the hospitality industry? (p. 287, Computer Usage @ Work)
- Who conceptualized the computer mouse more than 60 years ago? (p. 289, Technology Trailblazers)
- How to download music? (pp. 298–299 and Computer Concepts CourseMate, Learn How To)
- How to use the numeric keypad keys to move the mouse pointer, click, right-click, double-click, and drag? (Windows Exercises, Computer Concepts CourseMate)

For these answers and to discover much more information essential to this course, read Chapter 5 and visit the associated Computer Concepts CourseMate at www.cengagebrain.com.

Customize Your Learning Experience

Q & A

How can I meet one or more of these goals?

Make use of the goal's resources for each chapter in the book and you should meet that goal by the end of the course.

Adapt this book to meet your needs by determining your goal. Would you like to be an informed digital consumer? A productive technology user? A safe user, protected from the risks in a digital world? A competent digital citizen? A future entrepreneur or professional in a digital society?

Every chapter in this Student Success Guide identifies resources targeted toward each of these goals, along with criteria to verify you understand the resources' content. Resources may be located in the textbook, on the Computer Concepts CourseMate Web site, in the interactive eBook, and on the Web.

Informed Digital Consumer

Goal: I would like to understand the terminology used in Web or print advertisements that sell computers, mobile devices, and related technology, as well as the jargon used by sales associates in computer or electronics stores, so that I can make informed purchasing decisions.

Topic	Resource	Location	Now you should . . .
Keyboard Types	Text/Figures	pp. 260–262	Know keyboard types including enhanced, gaming, and wireless
Mouse Types	Text/Figures	pp. 263–264	Know mouse types including optical, laser, air, and wireless
Portable Media Player	FAQ	p. 267	Know which companies sell the most portable media players
Smart Phone	Text/Figure	pp. 268–269	Be familiar with various types of input for smart phones

Continued on next page

Continued from previous page

Topic	Resource	Location	Now you should . . .
Game Controllers	Text/Figures	pp. 270–271	Be able to identify and know the purpose of various game controllers
	Drag and Drop Figure 5-19	eBook p. 270 or CourseMate	
	Web Link		Know about the Wii Remote
	Video		Know about the xBox Kinect
Digital Camera Types	Text	p. 272	Know the differences of studio, field, and point-and-shoot cameras
Resolution	Text/Figure	p. 273	Be able to explain resolution and its relationship to digital cameras
Web Cams	Text/Figure	pp. 275–276	Know the purpose and approximate costs of Web cams
Flatbed Scanner	Text	p. 278	Know flatbed scanner resolutions
Bar Code Reader	Video	eBook p. 280 or CourseMate	Be familiar with the benefits of a bar code reader
Fingerprint Reader	Text/Figure	p. 282	Be familiar with features and costs of fingerprint readers
Terminals	Text/Figures	pp. 284–285	Know the purpose and uses of POS terminals, ATMs, and DVD kiosks
Input Device Recommendations	Text/Figure	p. 285	Be familiar with input device recommendations for various users
Logitech	Text	p. 289	Be familiar with Logitech's recent products
	Link	eBook p. 289 or CourseMate	
Nokia	Text	p. 289	Be familiar with Nokia's recent products
	Link	eBook p. 289 or CourseMate	

Productive Technology User

Goal: I would like to learn ways that technology can benefit me at home, work, and school. I also would like to learn helpful techniques for using technology so that I can perform tasks more efficiently and be more productive in daily activities.

Topic	Resource	Location	Now you should . . .
Keyboard Keys	Text/Figure	pp. 260–261	Be able to identify and know the function of various keyboard keys
	Drag and Drop Figure 5-2	eBook p. 261 or CourseMate	
	Windows Exercises	CourseMate	Be able to use Windows to customize a keyboard, use mouse keys, and open the on-screen keyboard
Mobile Computer and Device Keyboards	Text/Figure	pp. 262–263	Know the types of keyboards on notebook computers and mobile devices and the advantage of predictive text input
	Drag and Drop Figure 5-5	eBook p. 263 or CourseMate	
Using a Mouse	Text/Figure	p. 264	Know how to use a mouse
	Drag and Drop Figure 5-8	eBook p. 264 or CourseMate	
Other Pointing Devices	Text/Figures	pp. 265–266	Know the look and purpose of a trackball, touchpad, and pointing stick
Touch Screens	Text/Figures	pp. 266–267	Know the function of touch screens and their various uses
	Web Link	eBook p. 266 or CourseMate	Be familiar with various multi-touch screen uses
Touch-Sensitive Pads	Text/Figure	p. 267	Know the functions of a touch-sensitive pad and its uses

Continued on next page

Continued from previous page

Topic	Resource	Location	Now you should . . .
Stylus and Digital Pen	Text/Figure	p. 268	Be familiar with uses of a stylus and digital pen
Digital Camera Use	Text/Figure and FAQ	pp. 272–273	Know ways users work with images from a digital camera and how a digital camera works
	Figure 5-20 Animation	eBook p. 272 or CourseMate	
Voice Input	Text/Figure	p. 274	Know the uses of voice input and how voice recognition works
Audio Input	Text/Figure	pp. 274–275	Know uses of audio input and ports used to connect music devices
	Innovative Computing	p. 275	Be familiar with music production software
	Link	eBook p. 275 or CourseMate	
	Labs	CourseMate	Know how to import and download audio files, and burn audio CDs
	Learn How To	pp. 298–299 and CourseMate	Know how to download songs to a portable media player
DV Cameras	Text/Figure	p. 275	Know how users work with digital video cameras
Web Cam	Learn How To	p. 298 and CourseMate	Know how to install and use a Web cam
Video Editing	Video	At the Movies, CourseMate	Know how to edit videos, import clips, and work with clips and transitions
	Labs	CourseMate	
Health Video Conference	Innovative Computing	p. 276	Be familiar with an example of how patients video conference with medical professionals
	Link	eBook p. 276 or CourseMate	
Flatbed Scanner	Text/Figure	p. 278	Know how flatbed scanners work and the benefit of OCR software
Scanning	FAQ	p. 278	Be familiar with how to use a scanner
	FAQ Link	eBook p. 278, or Scanning link, CourseMate	
Input Devices	Windows Exercises	CourseMate	Be able to use Windows to identify input devices on a computer
Photo Editing	Web Apps	CourseMate	Be able to upload photos to Flickr, crop them, and share them

Safe User, Protected from the Risks in a Digital World

Goal: I would like to take measures to (1) protect my computers, devices, and data from loss, damage, or misuse; (2) minimize or prevent risks associated with using technology; and (3) minimize the environmental impact of using computers and related devices.

Topic	Resource	Location	Now you should . . .
Keyboard Monitors	Ethics & Issues	p. 261	Recognize how your keystrokes can be logged and monitored
Keyboard Ergonomics	Text/Figure	p. 262	Know the purpose and design of an ergonomic keyboard
Ergonomics	Web Link	eBook p. 262 or CourseMate	Be familiar with the latest information regarding ergonomics
RSIs	FAQ	p. 263	Know ways to reduce your chance of experiencing RSIs and recognize the symptoms
	Link and Video	eBook p. 262 or CourseMate	
	Ethics & Issues	p. 265	Know the issues surrounding workplace RSIs

Continued on next page

Continued from previous page

Topic	Resource	Location	Now you should . . .
Mobile Device Threats	FAQ	p. 269	Be familiar with threats to mobile computers and devices
Medical Advice	Ethics & Issues	p. 271	Be familiar with issues of video game makers providing medical advice
RFID Tracking	Ethics & Issues	p. 280	Be aware of privacy issues surrounding RFID use
Biometric Monitoring	Ethics & Issues	p. 283	Be aware of privacy issues surrounding biometric facial recognition
	Video	eBook p. 283 or CourseMate	

Competent Digital Citizen

Goal: I would like to be knowledgeable and well-informed about computers, mobile devices, and related technology, so that I am digitally literate in my personal and professional use of digital devices.

Topic	Resource	Location	Now you should . . .
Input	Text/Figure	pp. 258–259	Know the difference among a program, command, and user response
Key Arrangement	FAQ	p. 261	Know the rationale for the arrangement of keyboard typing keys
	FAQ Link	eBook p. 261, or Keyboards link, CourseMate	
Pointing Device	Text	p. 261 Figure 5-3 and p. 263	Know the purpose of a pointing device and its relationship to a pointer
Scanners	Text/Figure	p. 277	Know the various types of scanners and their primary uses
	Drag and Drop Figure 5-27	eBook p. 277 or CourseMate	
Optical Readers	Text/Figures	p. 279	Know the difference between OCR and OMR
Bar Code Readers	Text/Figure	p. 280	Know the purpose of bar code readers and uses of bar codes
RFID Readers	Text/Figure	pp. 280–281	Know the purpose of RFID readers and uses of RFID tags
Magstripe Reader	Text/Figure	p. 281	Know the purpose of magstripe readers and what is stored in stripes
MICR	Text/Figure	p. 281	Know the purpose of MICR readers and what they read on a check
Biometric Input	Text/Figure	pp. 282–283	Know the purpose and uses of various biometric devices
	Video	eBook p. 288 or CourseMate	
	Text	p. 288	Be familiar with the process of authentication in finger-scan and other biometric technology
	Link	eBook p. 288 or CourseMate	
Input Devices for Physically Challenged Users	Text/Figures	p. 286	Be familiar with the ADA and input devices designed to assist users who are physically challenged
	Looking Ahead		
	Video and Link	eBook p. 286 or CourseMate	
Gesture Recognition	Text	p. 286	Be familiar with the purpose and uses of gesture recognition
	Web Link	eBook p. 286 or CourseMate	
Satoru Iwata	Text	p. 289	Be familiar with Satoru Iwata's accomplishments at Nintendo
	Link and Video	eBook p. 289 or CourseMate	
Douglas Engelbart	Text	p. 289	Be familiar with Douglas Engelbart's contribution to the computing industry
	Link	eBook p. 289 or CourseMate	

Future Entrepreneur or Professional in a Digital Society

Goal: As I ponder my future, I envision myself as an entrepreneur or skilled professional using technology to support my business endeavors or job responsibilities. Along the way, I may interact with a variety of computer professionals — or I may just become one myself!

Topic	Resource	Location	Now you should . . .
Signature Capture Pads	Web Link	eBook p. 268 or CourseMate	Be able to describe signature capture pads, along with their features and costs
Graphics Tablet	Text/Figure	p. 268	Know how professionals use a graphics tablet
Web Cams	Text	pp. 275–276	Know how businesses might use a Web cam
	Web Link	eBook p. 276 or CourseMate	
Video Conference	Text/Figure	pp. 276–277	Know what is required for a video conference and how it works, and give examples of its uses
	Innovative Computing Video	eBook p. 276 or CourseMate	
Bar Code Readers	Web Link	eBook p. 280 or CourseMate	Be familiar with features and prices of bar code readers
RFID Readers	Text	p. 280	Know why some retailers prefer RFID to bar code technology
Data Collection	Text/Figure	p. 282	Be familiar with uses of data collection devices
Computers in Hospitality Industry	Computer Usage @ Work	p. 287	Recognize how personnel and customers use computers in hotels and restaurants
	Link and Video	eBook p. 287 or CourseMate	
Data Entry Clerk	Exploring Computer Careers	CourseMate	Be familiar with the responsibilities of and education required for a data entry clerk

Preparing for a Test

Visit the Computer Concepts CourseMate at www.cengagebrain.com and then navigate to the Chapter 5 Web Apps resource for this book to prepare for your test.

Does your class use the Computer Concepts CourseMate Web site? If so, prepare for your test by using the Flash Cards, Study Guide, and Practice Test Web apps — available for your smart phone or tablet.

If your class does not use the Computer Concepts CourseMate Web site or you prefer to use your book, you can prepare for the test by doing the Quiz Yourself activities on pages 271, 277, and 287; reading the Chapter Review on pages 290–291; ensuring you know the definitions for the terms on page 292; and completing the Checkpoint exercises on pages 293–294. You also should know the material identified in the Chapter 5 Study Guide that follows.

Chapter 5 Study Guide

This study guide identifies material you should know for the Chapter 5 exam. You may want to write the answers in a notebook, enter them on your digital device, record them into a phone, or highlight them in your book. Choose whichever method helps you remember the best.

1. Define the terms, input and input device.

2. Differentiate among a program, command, and user response.

3. Describe the arrangement of keys on an enhanced keyboard, and identify the function of commonly used keys and buttons on desktop computer keyboards.

4. Explain the purpose of keyboard monitoring software.

5. Identify two types of wireless technologies that a wireless keyboard or wireless mouse might use.

6. The goal of _____ is to incorporate comfort, efficiency, and safety in the design of the workplace.

7. Identify ways to reduce chances of experiencing RSIs.

8. Describe how keyboards for mobile computers and devices differ from desktop computer keyboards.

9. Describe the function and purpose of predictive text input.

10. Identify the purpose of a pointing device and its relationship to a pointer.

Continued on next page

Continued from previous page

11. Describe the differences among mouse types: optical mouse, laser mouse, air mouse, and wireless mouse.

12. Explain how to use a mouse and common mouse operations.

13. Describe a trackball, touchpad, and pointing stick.

14. Identify uses of touch screens.

15. Touch screens that recognize multiple points of contact at the same time are known as _____.

16. Explain how to use a touch-sensitive pad.

17. Describe various types of pen input.

18. Identify various types of input for smart phones.

19. Identify security risks for mobile computers and devices.

20. Summarize the purpose of various game controllers: gamepads, joysticks and wheels, light guns, dance pads, and motion-sensing game controllers.

21. Differentiate among types of digital cameras: studio, field, and point-and-shoot.

22. Explain how resolution affects the quality of a picture captured on a digital camera.

23. MP stands for _____.

24. Differentiate between optical and enhanced resolution.

25. Describe the uses of voice input.

26. Explain the purpose of music production software.

27. Describe a DV camera.

28. Identify the purpose of a Web cam.

29. Describe how a video conference works.

30. Differentiate among flatbed, pen, sheet-fed, and drum scanners. State ways to improve scanned document quality.

31. Identify the purpose of OCR software.

32. Describe how optical readers work. Differentiate between OCR and OMR. Give examples of their uses.

33. Describe how bar code readers work. Identify uses of bar codes.

34. Describe how RFID readers work. State uses of RFID tags.

35. Identify privacy issues surrounding use of RFID.

36. Identify the purpose of magstripe readers. State types of information stored on a stripe.

37. The _____ industry almost exclusively uses MICR readers.

38. Give examples where data collection devices are used.

39. Define the term, biometrics. Give examples of biometric identifiers.

40. Describe the purpose and use of these biometric devices: fingerprint reader, face recognition system, hand geometry system, voice verification system, signature verification system, and iris recognition system.

41. Identify privacy issues surrounding biometric face recognition systems.

42. Identify the purpose of POS terminals, ATMs, and DVD kiosks.

43. PIN stands for _____.

44. Briefly describe the Americans with Disabilities Act.

45. Identify input devices for physically challenged users.

46. Describe how restaurants and hotels use computers.

47. Briefly explain the enrollment and matching steps in biometric technology.

48. Identify types of devices sold by Logitech.

Check This Out

As technology changes, you must keep up with updates, new products, breakthroughs, and recent advances to remain digitally literate. The list below identifies topics related to this chapter that you should explore to keep current. In parentheses beside each topic, you will find a search term to help begin your research using a search engine, such as Google.

1. **new virtual keyboards** (search for: virtual keyboard)
2. **recent keyboard monitoring software hacking** (search for: keylogging)
3. **health injuries resulting from using tablet computers** (search for: tablet ergonomics)
4. **new pointing devices** (search for: latest pointing devices)
5. **latest Microsoft Surface table** (search for: Microsoft Surface)
6. **input devices for smart phones** (search for: new smart phone input devices)
7. **popular game controllers** (search for: game controllers)
8. **input accessories for the Xbox** (search for: Xbox accessories)
9. **3-D motion control input device** (search for: 3D motion controller)
10. **digital camera features** (search for: digital camera specification review)
11. **smart phone voice recognition technology** (search for: smart phone input speech)
12. **features of new 3-D digital video cameras** (search for: 3D video camera)
13. **video conferencing on mobile devices** (search for: mobile device video conferencing)
14. **popular types of 2-D bar codes** (search for: 2D bar codes)
15. **mobile payments made using fingerprint scanning technology** (search for: mobile payment fingerprint)

For current news and information
Check us out on Facebook and Twitter. See your instructor or the Computer Concepts CourseMate for specific information.

Student Success Guide

Output

Why Should I Learn About Output Devices?

"On Sunday afternoons, I relax by watching sports on my 60-inch HDTV. My wireless surround sound system makes me feel like I am sitting in the stadium's front-row seat. I even have produced flyers on my ink-jet printer inviting my friends to watch playoff games with me. What other output devices could I possibly use?"

True, you may be familiar with some of the material in this chapter, but do you know . . .

"What other output devices could I possibly use?"

- Which features to consider when purchasing an LCD screen or monitor? (pp. 308–309, LCD Quality)
- How ink-jet printers form characters and graphics on paper? (pp. 316–317, Ink-Jet Printers)
- Where you can discard depleted toner cartridges in an environmentally safe manner? (p. 320, FAQ)
- How 3-D graphics are generated for video games? (p. 330, High-Tech Talk)
- Who helped build the first desktop computer and was on the cover of *Time* magazine by age 26? (p. 331, Technology Trailblazers)
- How to make a video and upload it to YouTube? (pp. 340–341 and Computer Concepts CourseMate, Learn How To)
- How to use video editing software? (p. 348, Digital Video Technology Special Feature)
- Which Windows options assist those with hearing or visual impairments? (Windows Exercises, Computer Concepts CourseMate)

For these answers and to discover much more information essential to this course, read Chapter 6 and visit the associated Computer Concepts CourseMate at www.cengagebrain.com.

Q&A How can I meet one or more of these goals?

Make use of the goal's resources for each chapter in the book and you should meet that goal by the end of the course.

Customize Your Learning Experience

Adapt this book to meet your needs by determining your goal. Would you like to be an informed digital consumer? A productive technology user? A safe user, protected from the risks in a digital world? A competent digital citizen? A future entrepreneur or professional in a digital society?

Every chapter in this Student Success Guide identifies resources targeted toward each of these goals, along with criteria to verify you understand the resources' content. Resources may be located in the textbook, on the Computer Concepts CourseMate Web site, in the interactive eBook, and on the Web.

Informed Digital Consumer

Goal: I would like to understand the terminology used in Web or print advertisements that sell computers, mobile devices, and related technology, as well as the jargon used by sales associates in computer or electronics stores, so that I can make informed purchasing decisions.

Topic	Resource	Location	Now you should . . .
LCD Monitors and Screens	Text/Figures	pp. 307–309	Be familiar with features of LCD monitors and screens
	Web Link	eBook p. 307 or CourseMate	
	Video	At the Movies, CourseMate	
Digital Frames	Innovative Computing	p. 308	Be familiar with features and costs of digital frames
	Link and Video	eBook p. 308 or CourseMate	
LCD Quality	Text/Figure and FAQ	pp. 308–310	Know how resolution, response time, brightness, dot pitch, and contrast ratio affect quality of an LCD monitor or screen

Continued on next page

Continued from previous page

Topic	Resource	Location	Now you should . . .
Video Standards	Text/Figure	pp. 310–311	Know the video standards and typical resolutions for display devices
Plasma Monitors	Text/Figure	p. 311	Be familiar with features of plasma monitors
HDTV	Text/Figure	p. 312	Know the benefits of HDTV
Printer Purchase	Text/Figure	p. 314	Be familiar with questions to ask when purchasing a printer
Ink-Jet Printers	Text/Figures	pp. 316–317	Know the features, resolution, costs, and uses of ink-jet printers and ink
Photo Printers	Text/Figure	p. 318	Know the features, costs, and uses of photo printers
	Web Link	eBook p. 318 or CourseMate	
Photo Paper	FAQ	p. 318	Be familiar with paper to use for photo printing
	FAQ Link	eBook p. 318, or Photo Paper link, CourseMate	
Laser Printers	Text/Figure	pp. 319–320	Know the features, costs, and uses of laser printers and toner
Multifunction Peripherals	Text/Figure	pp. 320–321	Know the features, advantages, and disadvantages of multifunction peripherals
Digital Photo Printer	Text/Figure	p. 321	Know the features of digital photo printers for home use
Speakers	Text/Figure	pp. 323–324	Be familiar with features and types of speakers, configurations of surround sound systems, and audio resolution
Headphones and Earbuds	Text/Figures	pp. 324–325	Understand the difference between headphones, headsets, and earbuds
	Web Link	eBook p. 324 or CourseMate	
Game Controllers	Text/Figure	pp. 326–327	Know the purpose of force-feedback game controllers
Output Device Recommendations	Text/Figure	p. 327	Be familiar with output device recommendations for various users
HP	Text	p. 331	Be familiar with HP's products and services
	Link	eBook p. 331 or CourseMate	
Samsung	Text	p. 331	Be familiar with Samsung's products
	Link	eBook p. 331 or CourseMate	
Digital Video Technology	Text/Figures	pp. 344–349	Know how to select a video camera, record a video, transfer and manage videos, edit videos, and distribute videos
	Figure 6-3 Animation	p. 346	
	Drag and Drop Figure 6-6	p. 347	

Productive Technology User

Goal: I would like to learn ways that technology can benefit me at home, work, and school. I also would like to learn helpful techniques for using technology so that I can perform tasks more efficiently and be more productive in daily activities.

Topic	Resource	Location	Now you should . . .
Monitors	Text	p. 306	Know the adjustments available on computer monitors
Graphics Ports	Text/Figure	pp. 310–311	Be familiar with the purpose of DVI, HDMI, and other graphics ports
	Drag and Drop Figure 6-6		
	Web Link	eBook p. 310 or CourseMate	

Continued on next page

Continued from previous page

Topic	Resource	Location	Now you should . . .
Hard Copy Output	Text/Figures	pp. 313–314	Understand the difference between portrait and landscape orientation
Printing Methods	Text/Figure	pp. 314–315	Be familiar with the various printing methods
Wireless Printing	Text	pp. 314–315	Know the wireless technologies for printing
Accessibility Options	Windows Exercises	CourseMate	Know how to use Sound Sentry, Narrator, and Magnifier in Windows
Paint	Windows Exercises	CourseMate	Know how to use Paint
Sound	Windows Exercises	CourseMate	Know how to adjust sound in Windows
Make and Upload a Video	Learn How To	pp. 340–341 and CourseMate	Know how to transfer a video to a computer, upload the video to YouTube, and view the video
Control Printing	Learn How To	p. 341 and CourseMate	Know how to control printing on a Windows computer
Sending Files	Web Apps	CourseMate	Know how to use YouSendIt

Safe User, Protected from the Risks in a Digital World

Goal: I would like to take measures to (1) protect my computers, devices, and data from loss, damage, or misuse; (2) minimize or prevent risks associated with using technology; and (3) minimize the environmental impact of using computers and related devices.

Topic	Resource	Location	Now you should . . .
Computer Eye Strain	FAQ	p. 306	Know how to ease eyestrain while using a computer
	FAQ Link	eBook p. 306, or Eye Strain link, CourseMate	
Digital Billboards	Ethics & Issues	p. 306	Recognize the controversy surrounding digital billboards
Reusable Paper	Looking Ahead	p. 314	Know how reusable paper works
	Link and Video	eBook p. 314 or CourseMate	
Toner Disposal	FAQ	p. 320	Know how to dispose of toner cartridges properly
	FAQ Link and Video	eBook p. 320, or Recycling Toner Cartridges link, CourseMate	Be familiar with recycling guidelines
Green Graffiti	Ethics & Issues	p. 325	Be familiar with issues surrounding green graffiti
	Video	eBook p. 325 or CourseMate	

Competent Digital Citizen

Goal: I would like to be knowledgeable and well-informed about computers, mobile devices, and related technology, so that I am digitally literate in my personal and professional use of digital devices.

Topic	Resource	Location	Now you should . . .
Output	Text/Figure	pp. 304–305	Be able to identify various output devices and types of output
Display Devices	Text	p. 306	Be familiar with display devices on various computers and devices
	Labs	CourseMate	
LCD Technology	Text	p. 308	Know various types of LCD technology

Continued on next page

Continued from previous page

Topic	Resource	Location	Now you should . . .
Video Cards	Text	pp. 310–311	Know about bit depth and video memory on video cards
Video Content	FAQ	p. 311	Know the type of video content most often viewed
	FAQ Link	eBook p. 311, or Video Output Content link, CourseMate	Know about video apps
Largest HDTV	FAQ	p. 312	Be familiar with specs for the largest HDTV
	FAQ Link	eBook p. 312, or Largest High-Definition Display link, CourseMate	
CRT Monitors	Text/Figure	p. 313	Know how CRT monitors work and that their popularity has declined
Nonimpact Printers	Text	p. 315	Describe how nonimpact printers work and name examples
	Labs	CourseMate	
Ink-Jet Printers	Text/Figure	pp. 316–317	Know how ink-jet printers work
	Drag and Drop Figure 6-16	eBook p. 317 or CourseMate	
	Web Link		
Laser Printers	Text/Figure	p. 320	Know how laser printers work
	Drag and Drop Figure 6-19	eBook p. 320 or CourseMate	
	Web Link		
Output Devices for Physically Challenged	Text/Figures	pp. 328–329	Be familiar output devices designed to assist users who are physically challenged
	Ethics & Issues		
Computers in Space Exploration	Computer Usage @ Work	p. 329	Recognize how computers are used in space exploration
	Link and Video	eBook p. 329 or CourseMate	
Steve Jobs	Text	p. 331	Be familiar with Steve Jobs's impact on the computing industry and his accomplishments
	Video	eBook p. 331 or CourseMate	
Ursula Burns	Text	p. 331	Know the company of which Ursula Burns is chair and CEO
	Link	eBook p. 331 or CourseMate	

Future Entrepreneur or Professional in a Digital Society

Goal: As I ponder my future, I envision myself as an entrepreneur or skilled professional using technology to support my business endeavors or job responsibilities. Along the way, I may interact with a variety of computer professionals — or I may just become one myself!

Topic	Resource	Location	Now you should . . .
Thermal Printers	Text/Figure	p. 321	Know the uses of thermal printers in businesses
Mobile Printers	Text/Figure	p. 321	Know the features and technology used in mobile printers
Label and Postage Printers	Text/Figure	p. 322	Know the functions of label and postage printers

Continued on next page

Continued from previous page

Topic	Resource	Location	Now you should . . .
Plotters and Large-Format Printers	Text/Figure	p. 322	Know the features, technology, costs, and uses of plotters and large-format printers
	Web Link	eBook p. 322 or CourseMate	
	Figure 6-24 Video		
Impact Printers	Text/Figure	pp. 322–323	Know how impact printers work, and uses of dot-matrix and line printers
Data Projectors	Text/Figure	pp. 325–326	Know the function and types of data projectors
Interactive Whiteboards	Text/Figure	p. 326	Know the function, technologies, and uses of interactive whiteboards
	Web Link and Video	eBook p. 326 or CourseMate	
3-D Graphics	Text	p. 330	Know how professionals, such as game programmers, create 3-D graphics, and how 3-D graphics work
	Link and Video	eBook p. 330 or CourseMate	
	Labs	CourseMate	
Graphic Designer/ Illustrator	Exploring Computer Careers	CourseMate	Be familiar with the responsibilities of and education required for a graphic designer/illustrator

Preparing for a Test

Visit the Computer Concepts CourseMate at **www.cengagebrain.com** and then navigate to the Chapter 6 Web Apps resource for this book to prepare for your test.

Does your class use the Computer Concepts CourseMate Web site? If so, prepare for your test by using the Flash Cards, Study Guide, and Practice Test Web apps — available for your smart phone or tablet.

If your class does not use the Computer Concepts CourseMate Web site or you prefer to use your book, you can prepare for the test by doing the Quiz Yourself activities on pages 313, 323, and 329; reading the Chapter Review on pages 332–333; ensuring you know the definitions for the terms on page 334; and completing the Checkpoint exercises on pages 335–336. You also should know the material identified in the Chapter 6 Study Guide that follows.

Chapter 6 Study Guide

This study guide identifies material you should know for the Chapter 6 exam. You may want to write the answers in a notebook, enter them on your digital device, record them into a phone, or highlight them in your book. Choose whichever method helps you remember the best.

1. Define the terms, output and output device.
2. Describe the types of output: text, graphics, audio, and video.
3. Identify ways most monitors can be adjusted.
4. List ways to ease eyestrain while using a computer.
5. Describe a digital billboard.
6. LCD stands for _____.
7. Identify characteristics of LCD monitors and LCD screens.
8. Describe how LCD monitors and screens work.
9. Identify the advantages of active-matrix displays.
10. Describe the factors that affect the quality of an LCD monitor or LCD screen: resolution, response time, brightness, dot pitch, and contrast ratio.
11. Differentiate among these ports: DVI, HDMI, and S-video.
12. _____ defines a display's width relative to its height.
13. Explain the relationship of bit depth and video memory to video cards.
14. Explain the characteristics of plasma monitors.
15. Describe advantages of digital television signals over analog signals.
16. HDTV stands for _____.
17. Differentiate between portrait and landscape orientation.
18. Identify questions to ask when purchasing a printer.
19. Describe how reusable paper works.
20. Describe various ways to print.

Continued on next page

Continued from previous page

21. Differentiate between a nonimpact printer and an impact printer.

22. Describe characteristics and uses of ink-jet printers.

23. DPI stands for _____.

24. Describe characteristics of photo printers.

25. Describe characteristics and uses of laser printers. Identify proper ways to dispose of toner cartridges.

26. Identify the features, advantages, and disadvantage of multifunction peripherals.

27. Explain how thermal printers work. Give examples of their use.

28. Describe a mobile printer.

29. Describe how label and postage printers work.

30. Describe characteristics of plotters and large-format printers.

31. Describe the uses of speakers. Explain various surround sound system configurations.

32. Define the term, audio resolution.

33. Differentiate among headphones, earbuds, and headsets.

34. Identify the purpose of data projectors. Differentiate between LCD and DLP projectors.

35. Describe green graffiti.

36. Describe the purpose of interactive whiteboards and technologies for displaying computer images on them.

37. Describe how force-feed game controllers and tactile output work.

38. Identify output options for physically challenged users.

39. Explain a 3-D graphic. Identify the purpose of wireframes and considerations when adding surface to a wireframe.

40. Identify products manufactured by HP.

41. Identify products manufactured by Samsung.

42. _____ cofounded Apple with Steve Wozniak.

43. Describe how to transfer videos from a DV camera to a computer.

44. Name popular video file formats.

45. Explain ways to edit a video.

Check This Out

As technology changes, you must keep up with updates, new products, breakthroughs, and recent advances to remain digitally literate. The list below identifies topics related to this chapter that you should explore to keep current. In parentheses beside each topic, you will find a search term to help begin your research using a search engine, such as Google.

1. **top LCD monitors** (search for: LCD monitor reviews)

2. **latest plasma monitors** (search for: best plasma monitors)

3. **popular HDTV models** (search for: top high definition TVs)

4. **new wireless printers** (search for: wireless printers)

5. **best ink-jet printers** (search for: top ink jet printers)

6. **latest photo printer characteristics** (search for: photo printer features)

7. **new laser printers** (search for: latest laser printers)

8. **widely used multifunction products** (search for: multifunction peripherals)

9. **popular mobile printer features** (search for: top mobile printers)

10. **latest wireless speaker systems** (search for: wireless speakers)

11. **popular force-feedback game controllers** (search for: force feedback gaming accessories)

12. **new output devices for physically challenged users** (search for: output devices physically challenged)

13. **3-D graphics creation** (search for: new 3D technology)

14. **Steve Jobs's influence on consumer technology** (search for: Steve Jobs legacy)

15. **latest digital video technology** (search for: digital video equipment)

For current news and information
Check us out on Facebook and Twitter. See your instructor or the Computer Concepts CourseMate for specific information.

Storage

Why Should I Learn About Storage?

"My USB flash drive stores all the files I need for my classes. I transfer all of my digital photos from an SD card to my computer's hard disk, which also has plenty of space for my programs and music. Weekly, I back up files on my computer to an external hard disk. What other types of storage could I need?"

True, you may be familiar with some of the material in this chapter, but do you know . . .

"What other types of storage could I need?"

- How your hard disk reads and writes data? (p. 358, How a Hard Disk Works)
- How to safeguard data on your mobile media when traveling on commercial aircraft? (p. 367, FAQ)
- Where you can save and share your audio, video, graphics, and other important files on the Internet? (pp. 368–369, Cloud Storage)
- When law enforcement officials may read your e-mail messages? (p. 369, Ethics & Issues)
- How meteorologists use computers to forecast storms and hurricanes? (p. 381, Computer Usage @ Work)
- Which company developed the first hard disk for the personal computer? (p. 383, Companies on the Cutting Edge)
- How to increase space on your hard disk? (p. 392 and Computer Concepts CourseMate, Learn How To)
- How to recover a file you deleted accidentally? (Windows Exercises, Computer Concepts CourseMate)

For these answers and to discover much more information essential to this course, read Chapter 7 and visit the associated Computer Concepts CourseMate at www.cengagebrain.com.

Customize Your Learning Experience

Q&A | How can I meet one or more of these goals?

Make use of the goal's resources for each chapter in the book and you should meet that goal by the end of the course.

Adapt this book to meet your needs by determining your goal. Would you like to be an informed digital consumer? A productive technology user? A safe user, protected from the risks in a digital world? A competent digital citizen? A future entrepreneur or professional in a digital society?

Every chapter in this Student Success Guide identifies resources targeted toward each of these goals, along with criteria to verify you understand the resources' content. Resources may be located in the textbook, on the Computer Concepts CourseMate Web site, in the interactive eBook, and on the Web.

Informed Digital Consumer

Goal: I would like to understand the terminology used in Web or print advertisements that sell computers, mobile devices, and related technology, as well as the jargon used by sales associates in computer or electronics stores, so that I can make informed purchasing decisions.

Topic	Resource	Location	Now you should . . .
Storage Capacity	Text/Figure	p. 354	Know terms and abbreviations that define capacity of storage media
	Drag and Drop Figure 7-2	eBook p. 354 or CourseMate	
Transfer Rate	Text/Figure	p. 355 and p. 358	Be familiar with storage media transfer rates and relative speed compared to memory
	Drag and Drop Figure 7-4	eBook p. 355 or CourseMate	
Hard Disks	Text	pp. 355–356	Know the purpose of hard disks, their capacities, and uses

Continued on next page

Continued from previous page

Topic	Resource	Location	Now you should . . .
RAID	Text	p. 360	Know the purpose of RAID
External Hard Disks	Text/Figures	pp. 360–361	Know the capacities and advantages of external and removable hard disks
Hard Disk Controllers	Text	pp. 361–362	Know the differences of SATA, EIDE, SCSI, and SAS controllers
	Web Link	eBook p. 361 or CourseMate	
SSDs	Text/Figure and FAQ	p. 363	Know the purpose, form factors, capacities, speeds, advantages, and disadvantages of solid state drives
	FAQ Link	eBook p. 363, or Project Quicksilver link, CourseMate	
	Web Link	eBook p. 363 or CourseMate	
Memory Cards	Text/Figures	pp. 364–366	Know the types, capacities, and uses of various memory cards
	Web Link	eBook p. 365 or CourseMate	
USB Flash Drives	Text/Figure	p. 367	Know the uses and capacities of USB flash drives
ExpressCard Modules	Text/Figure	p. 367	Know the uses and sizes of ExpressCard modules
Optical Discs	Text/Figure	p. 370	Know the uses and sizes of optical discs
Optical Disc Types	Text/Figure	p. 372	Know the various optical disc formats and their capabilities
	Drag and Drop Figure 7-29	eBook p. 372 or CourseMate	
	Innovative Computing Link		
CDs	Text/Figure	pp. 372–373	Know the purpose and capacities of CD media and their drive speeds
Archive Disc	Text/Figure	p. 374	Know the use and cost of an archive disc or Picture CD
DVDs	Text/Figures and FAQ	pp. 375–376	Know the use and storage capacities of various DVD media
Blu-Ray	Text/Figure	p. 375	Know the use and storage capacities of Blu-ray media
	Web Link	eBook p. 375 or CourseMate	
Seagate	Text	p. 383	Be familiar with Seagate's products
	Link and Video	eBook p. 383 or CourseMate	
SanDisk	Text	p. 383	Be familiar with SanDisk's products
	Link	eBook p. 383 or CourseMate	

Productive Technology User

Goal: I would like to learn ways that technology can benefit me at home, work, and school. I also would like to learn helpful techniques for using technology so that I can perform tasks more efficiently and be more productive in daily activities.

Topic	Resource	Location	Now you should . . .
Miniature Hard Disks	Text/Figures	p. 361	Know the uses of miniature hard disks
Cloud Storage	Text/Figures	pp. 368–369	Know the purpose, advantages, services offered, and providers of cloud storage
	Innovative Computing	p. 368	
	Link and Video	eBook p. 368 or CourseMate	
	Web Link	eBook p. 369 or CourseMate	

Continued on next page

Continued from previous page

Topic	Resource	Location	Now you should . . .
Optical Discs	Text	p. 370	Know the use of LightScribe technology and drive designations
Archive Discs	Figure	p. 374	Know how an archive disc works
Converting to DVD	FAQ Link	eBook p. 376, or Transferring Movies link, CourseMate	Know about converting VHS to DVD
Managing Files and Folders; Hard Disks	Labs and Windows Exercises	CourseMate	Know how to use Windows to work with folders, to delete and restore files, and to learn statistics about the hard disk on a computer
TurboTax Online	Web Apps	CourseMate	Know how to use TurboTax Online to print and file a tax return

Safe User, Protected from the Risks in a Digital World

Goal: I would like to take measures to (1) protect my computers, devices, and data from loss, damage, or misuse; (2) minimize or prevent risks associated with using technology; and (3) minimize the environmental impact of using computers and related devices.

Topic	Resource	Location	Now you should . . .
Erasing Hard Disks	Ethics & Issues	p. 356	Be familiar with issues surrounding purchase of used hard disks
Crashes	Text/Figure	pp. 358–359	Know how to avoid a head crash
Disk Recovery	FAQ FAQ Link	p. 360 eBook p. 360, or Hard Disk Recovery link, CourseMate	Be familiar with how to recover a hard disk if it fails
	FAQ Video	eBook p. 360 or CourseMate	
Maintaining Hard Disk	Text and FAQ	p. 362	Know ways to maintain a hard disk: Check Disk, Cleanup Disk, and Defragment Disk
	Learn How To	pp. 392–393 and CourseMate	
	Labs and Windows Exercises	CourseMate	
Airport Screenings	FAQ	p. 367	Know how to safeguard data during air travel
	FAQ Link	eBook p. 367, or Airport Screening Equipment link, CourseMate	
Cloud Storage	Ethics & Issues	p. 369	Be familiar with privacy issues surrounding cloud storage
	Link and Video	eBook p. 369 or CourseMate	
Care for and Clean Discs	Text/Figure and FAQ	p. 371	Know how to care for, clean, and repair an optical disc
	FAQ Link	eBook p. 371, or Cleaning and Repairing Discs link, CourseMate	
Medical Records	Ethics & Issues	p. 380	Be aware of privacy issues surrounding medical records
Encrypting USB	Video	At the Movies, CourseMate	Know how to encrypt files on a USB flash drive
Recycle Bin	Windows Exercises	CourseMate	Know how to recover files from the Recycle Bin

Competent Digital Citizen

Goal: I would like to be knowledgeable and well-informed about computers, mobile devices, and related technology, so that I am digitally literate in my personal and professional use of digital devices.

Topic	Resource	Location	Now you should . . .
Program Storage	Text	p. 352	Know where application and system software are stored
Storage Media	Text/Figure	p. 353	Be able to state examples of storage media
Volatility	Text/Figure	p. 354	Understand the difference between volatile and nonvolatile storage
Access Time	Text	p. 355	Know what access time measures
Hard Disk Recording Methods	Text/Figures	p. 356	Know the difference between perpendicular and longitudinal recording
	Web Link	eBook p. 356 or CourseMate	
	Figure Video		
Hard Disk Characteristics and Trends	FAQ	p. 356	Be familiar with density, formatting, clusters, cylinders, platters, form factors, disk cache and other hard disk characteristics; how hard disks work; and trends related to hard disks
	FAQ Link	eBook p. 356, or Hard Disk Capacity link, CourseMate	
	Text	pp. 357–359	
	Figure 7-9 Animation	p. 358	
	Drag and Drop Figure 7-12	p. 359	
	FAQ Link	eBook p. 362, or Hard Disk Performance link, CourseMate	
Memory Cards	Text/Figure	p. 366	Know how a memory card works
Optical Discs	Text/Figure	pp. 370–371	Know how a laser reads data on an optical disc
Media Life	Figure	p. 378	Know the life expectancies of various media
	Drag and Drop Figure 7-38	eBook p. 378 or CourseMate	
Rosetta Project	Looking Ahead	p. 379	Know about the Rosetta Project's long-term storage
	Link and Video	eBook p. 379 or CourseMate	
Computers in Meteorology	Computer Usage @ Work	p. 381	Know how meteorologists use computers in weather forecasting and to predict storm patterns and paths
	Link and Video	eBook p. 381 or CourseMate	
DNS Servers	Text/Figure	p. 382	Know how devices on the Internet locate each other
	Drag and Drop Figure 7-41	eBook p. 382 or CourseMate	
	Link and Video		

Future Entrepreneur or Professional in a Digital Society

Goal: As I ponder my future, I envision myself as an entrepreneur or skilled professional using technology to support my business endeavors or job responsibilities. Along the way, I may interact with a variety of computer professionals — or I may just become one myself!

Topic	Resource	Location	Now you should . . .
NAS	Text/Figure	p. 360	Know the purpose, features, and costs of network attached storage
	Web Link	eBook p. 360 or CourseMate	
Tape	Text/Figure	p. 376	Know how businesses use tape storage and how it works

Continued on next page

Continued from previous page

Topic	Resource	Location	Now you should . . .
Magnetic Stripe Cards and Smart Cards	Text/Figure	p. 377	Know how businesses use magnetic stripe cards and smart cards and how they work
	Ethics & Issues		
	Web Link and Video	eBook p. 377 or CourseMate	
Microfilm, Microfiche	Text/Figure	p. 378	Know the purposes and uses of microfilm and microfiche
Enterprise Storage	Text/Figure	p. 379	Know how large businesses store data, information, and programs
	Web Link	eBook p. 379 or CourseMate	
Storage Recommendations	Text/Figure	p. 380	Be familiar with storage recommendations for various users
Computer Technician	Exploring Computer Careers	CourseMate	Be familiar with the responsibilities and education required for a computer technician

Preparing for a Test

Visit the Computer Concepts CourseMate at www.cengagebrain.com and then navigate to the Chapter 7 Web Apps resource for this book to prepare for your test.

Does your class use the Computer Concepts CourseMate Web site? If so, prepare for your test by using the Flash Cards, Study Guide, and Practice Test Web apps — available for your smart phone or tablet.

If your class does not use the Computer Concepts CourseMate Web site or you prefer to use your book, you can prepare for the test by doing the Quiz Yourself activities on pages 362, 369, and 381; reading the Chapter Review on pages 384–385; ensuring you know the definitions for the terms on page 386; and completing the Checkpoint exercises on pages 387–388. You also should know the material identified in the Chapter 7 Study Guide that follows.

Chapter 7 Study Guide

This study guide identifies material you should know for the Chapter 7 exam. You may want to write the answers in a notebook, enter them on your digital device, record them into a phone, or highlight them in your book. Choose whichever method helps you remember the best.

1. Differentiate between storage devices and storage media.

2. Define storage capacity. Know the terms and abbreviations used to define storage capacity.

3. Describe why most memory is considered volatile and most storage is considered nonvolatile.

4. Differentiate between writing and reading, with respect to storage media.

5. Describe what access time measures.

6. MBps stands for _____, and GBps stands for _____.

7. Define transfer rate. Know which storage media have faster transfer rates.

8. Describe a hard disk. Differentiate between a fixed disk and a portable disk.

9. Differentiate between longitudinal and perpendicular recording.

10. Describe the purpose of a wiping utility.

11. Describe the characteristics of an internal hard disk including capacity, platters, form factor, read/write heads, cylinders, sectors and tracks, revolutions per minute, transfer rate, access time, and density.

12. Explain how a hard disk works.

13. Describe what causes a head crash.

14. Define the term, backup.

15. Identify the purpose of disk cache.

16. A group of two or more integrated hard disks is called a(n) _____.

17. Discuss the purpose of network attached storage devices.

18. Differentiate between external hard disks and removable hard disks. Identify their advantages over fixed disks.

19. Identify devices that contain miniature hard disks.

20. Differentiate among hard disk controllers: SATA, EIDE, SCSI, and SAS.

Continued on next page

Continued from previous page

21. Identify Windows tools that can improve the performance on a hard disk.

22. Describe the purpose and advantages of solid state drives.

23. Differentiate among various types of memory cards.

24. Describe the function of a card reader/writer.

25. Identify advantages and capacities of USB flash drives.

26. Describe the purpose and shapes of ExpressCard modules.

27. Describe cloud storage, examples of services provided, and reasons to use cloud storage.

28. Describe the characteristics of optical discs.

29. Define LightScribe technology.

30. Explain how a laser reads data on an optical disc.

31. Identify guidelines for proper care of optical discs.

32. Explain how to clean an optical disc.

33. Describe a single-session disc.

34. State the typical storage capacity of a CD. Differentiate among a CD-ROM, a CD-R, and a CD-RW.

35. Explain why the speed of a CD-ROM drive is significant. Describe how manufacturers measure optical disc speed.

36. _____ is the process of writing on an optical disc.

37. Describe ripping, with respect to CDs.

38. Explain the purpose of an archive disc or Picture CD.

39. State the storage capacities of DVDs. Differentiate among DVD-ROMs, recordable DVDs, and rewritable DVDs.

40. Describe features of Blu-ray Discs and drives.

41. Describe tape storage and identify its primary use today.

42. Identify uses of magnetic stripe cards and smart cards.

43. Identify uses of microfilm and microfiche.

44. Order these media in terms of life expectancy, from shortest to longest: optical discs, solid state drives, magnetic disks, and microfilm.

45. Explain why an enterprise's storage needs may change.

46. Describe the types of standards set by HIPAA.

47. Explain how meteorologists use computers to predict the weather.

48. Name the company that has the rights to design, develop, manufacture, and market every type of flash memory card format.

Check This Out

As technology changes, you must keep up with updates, new products, breakthroughs, and recent advances to remain digitally literate. The list below identifies topics related to this chapter that you should explore to keep current. In parentheses beside each topic, you will find a search term to help begin your research using a search engine, such as Google.

1. **largest storage medium capacity** (search for: largest storage medium bytes)

2. **latest hard disk technologies** (search for: latest hard disks)

3. **popular failed hard disk data recovery methods** (search for: hard disk recovery software)

4. **widely used network attached storage devices** (search for: top network attached storage)

5. **new external hard disks** (search for: latest external hard disks)

6. **top removable hard disks** (search for: best removable hard disks)

7. **recent miniature hard disks** (search for: latest mini hard disks)

8. **widely used eSATA hard disk controllers** (search for: eSATA hard disk)

9. **popular solid state drives** (search for: top solid state drives)

10. **widely used memory cards** (search for: popular memory cards)

11. **innovative USB flash drives** (search for: latest USB flash drives)

12. **new ExpressCard modules** (search for: ExpressCard module growth)

13. **cloud storage developments** (search for: cloud storage news)

14. **latest Blu-ray Disc formats** (search for: new Blu-ray disc specifications)

15. **smart card technology advancements** (search for: smart card news)

For current news and information
Check us out on Facebook and Twitter. See your instructor or the Computer Concepts CourseMate for specific information.

Chapter 8

Operating Systems and Utility Programs

Why Should I Learn About Operating Systems and Utility Programs?

"My computer is running slower than when I bought it, but it seems to be working properly. I installed an antivirus program and update it and my Windows software occasionally. Aside from looking into ways to speed up my computer, why do I need to learn about operating systems and utility programs?"

True, you may be familiar with some of the material in this chapter, but do you know . . .

"Why do I need to learn about operating systems and utility programs?"

- Which combination of characters you should use to create a secure password? (p. 411, FAQ)
- Why a personal firewall may protect against unauthorized intrusions? (p. 425, Personal Firewall)
- What signs may indicate your computer is infected with a virus? (p. 425, Antivirus Programs)
- Who developed an operating system when he was a 21-year-old computer science student in Finland? (p. 431, Technology Trailblazers)
- How to update Windows regularly? (p. 440–441 and Computer Concepts CourseMate, Learn How To)
- How Windows can back up files? (Windows Exercises, Computer Concepts CourseMate)
- How to purchase a desktop or notebook computer, smart phone, portable media player, and digital camera? (p. 444–456, Buyer's Guide Special Feature)

For these answers and to discover much more information essential to this course, read Chapter 8 and visit the associated Computer Concepts CourseMate at www.cengagebrain.com.

Customize Your Learning Experience

Q & A

How can I meet one or more of these goals?

Make use of the goal's resources for each chapter in the book and you should meet that goal by the end of the course.

Adapt this book to meet your needs by determining your goal. Would you like to be an informed digital consumer? A productive technology user? A safe user, protected from the risks in a digital world? A competent digital citizen? A future entrepreneur or professional in a digital society?

Every chapter in this Student Success Guide identifies resources targeted toward each of these goals, along with criteria to verify you understand the resources' content. Resources may be located in the textbook, on the Computer Concepts CourseMate Web site, in the interactive eBook, and on the Web.

Informed Digital Consumer

Goal: I would like to understand the terminology used in Web or print advertisements that sell computers, mobile devices, and related technology, as well as the jargon used by sales associates in computer or electronics stores, so that I can make informed purchasing decisions.

Topic	Resource	Location	Now you should . . .
Platform	Text	p. 399	Know the meaning of a required platform on a software package
Aero Interface	Text/Figure	pp. 402–403	Know RAM requirements for Windows Aero vs. Windows 7 Basic
RAM	Text	p. 406	Know how to determine RAM requirements
Embedded Operating Systems	Text/Figures	pp. 418–421	Know the features of Windows Embedded CE, Windows Phone, iPhone OS, Blackberry, and Google Android
	Web Links	eBook p. 420 or CourseMate	
File Compression	Text	p. 427	Be familiar with file compression utilities and popular programs
	Web Link	eBook p. 427 or CourseMate	Be familiar with WinZip
Media Players	Text/Figure	pp. 427–428	Know the purpose of media players and popular players

Continued on next page

Continued from previous page

Topic	Resource	Location	Now you should . . .
Disc Burning	Text/Figure	p. 428	Know the purpose of disc burning software
Personal Computers	Text/Figure	p. 428	Know the purpose of personal computer maintenance utilities
RIM	Text	p. 431	Be familiar with RIM's products and services
	Link	eBook p. 431 or CourseMate	
Buyer's Guide	Text/Figures	pp. 444–456	Know some considerations when purchasing a desktop computer, notebook computer, smart phone, portable media player, and digital camera
	Drag and Drop Figure 8-2	eBook pp. 446–447 or CourseMate	
	Videos and Links	eBook p. 444, 450, 452, 454, and 456 or CourseMate	

Productive Technology User

Goal: I would like to learn ways that technology can benefit me at home, work, and school. I also would like to learn helpful techniques for using technology so that I can perform tasks more efficiently and be more productive in daily activities.

Topic	Resource	Location	Now you should . . .
Starting and Shutting Down a Computer	Text/Figure	p. 400	Know how to perform a cold boot, warm boot, restart, and shut down the computer
Boot Disk	Text	p. 402	Know the reason to have a boot or recovery disk
Shut Down Options	Text and FAQ	p. 402	Know the purpose of various options for shutting down a computer
	Web Link and FAQ Video	eBook p. 402 or CourseMate	
Windows User Interface	Drag and Drop Figure 8-4	eBook p. 403 or CourseMate	Know the elements of the Windows user interface
Foreground Program	Text	pp. 404–405	Know how to make a program active (in the foreground)
Thrashing	FAQ	p. 407	Know how to stop a computer from thrashing
	FAQ Link	eBook p. 407 or CourseMate	
Plug and Play	Text	p. 408	Know how Plug and Play works
USB Flash Drives	FAQ	p. 408	Know how to safely remove a USB flash drive
Network Connections	Text/Figure	p. 408	Know how to connect to a network using Windows
Performance	Text/Figure	pp. 408–409	Know how to monitor performance using Windows
Automatic Update	Text/Figure	pp. 409–410	Know the benefits of using automatic update
Passwords	Text/Figure FAQ	pp. 410–411	Know how to select a good password
	FAQ Link	eBook p. 411 or CourseMate	
Windows	Text/Figures	pp. 413–415	Know some features and editions of Windows 7
	Web Link and Figure Video	eBook p. 414 or CourseMate	
	Windows Exercises	CourseMate	Know how to determine the Windows version on a computer
	Learn How To	pp. 440–441 and CourseMate	Know how to keep Windows up-to-date
Mac OS X	Text/Figure	p. 415	Know some features of Mac OS X
	Link and Video	eBook p. 415 or CourseMate	

Continued on next page

Continued from previous page

Topic	Resource	Location	Now you should . . .
UNIX	Text/Figure	p. 417	Know some features of UNIX
Linux	Text	pp. 416–417	Know some features of Linux
	Web Link	eBook p. 417 or CourseMate	
File Manager	Text/Figure	p. 422	Know the purpose of a file manager
Search Utility	Text/Figure	p. 422	Know the purpose of a search utility
Image Viewer	Text/Figure	p. 423	Know the purpose of an image viewer
Uninstaller	Text and FAQ	p. 423	Know the purpose of an uninstaller and how to delete a program properly
	FAQ Link	eBook p. 423 or CourseMate	
	Labs	CourseMate	
Disk Cleanup	Text/Figure	p. 423	Know the purpose of a disk cleanup utility
Disk Defragmenter	Text/Figure	pp. 423–424	Know the purpose of a disk defragmenter utility
	Figure 8-32 Animation	eBook p. 424 or CourseMate	
Backup and Restore	Text/Figure	p. 424	Know the purpose of a backup and a restore utility and how to use Windows Backup and Restore
	Windows Exercises	CourseMate	
Screen Saver	Text/Figure	p. 425	Know the purpose of a screen saver and how to use one
	Windows Exercises	CourseMate	
Burning Video Discs	Web Link	eBook p. 428 or CourseMate	Know how to use RealPlayer to burn a video disc
	Learn How To	p. 440 and CourseMate	Know how to use Windows Explorer to burn a disc
Verisign	Text	p. 431	Be familiar with Verisign's services
	Link	eBook p. 431 or CourseMate	
Install and Maintain	Learn How To	p. 440 and CourseMate	Be familiar with how to install and maintain a computer
Photo Editing	Web Apps	CourseMate	Know how to use Photoshop Express to edit and share photos

Safe User, Protected from the Risks in a Digital World

Goal: I would like to take measures to (1) protect my computers, devices, and data from loss, damage, or misuse; (2) minimize or prevent risks associated with using technology; and (3) minimize the environmental impact of using computers and related devices.

Topic	Resource	Location	Now you should . . .
Automatic Update	Ethics & Issues	p. 410	Be aware of controversial issues surrounding automatic updates
Recover Deleted Files	Innovative Computing	p. 421	Be familiar with utilities that enable you to recover deleted files
	Link and Video	eBook p. 421 or CourseMate	
Personal Firewall	Text/Figure	p. 425	Know how a personal firewall can protect your computer
Antivirus Programs	Text/Figures	pp. 425–426	Know how antivirus programs protect your computer

Continued on next page

Continued from previous page

Topic	Resource	Location	Now you should . . .
Computer Viruses	FAQ	p. 426	Recognize signs of virus infection and steps to prevent computer virus infection
	FAQ Link	eBook p. 426 or CourseMate	
	Video	At the Movies, CourseMate	
	Labs	CourseMate	
Spyware Removers	Text	p. 426	Know the purpose of spyware and adware removers
Internet Filters	Text and FAQ	pp. 426–427	Know the purpose of Web filters, anti-spam programs, phishing filters, and pop-up blockers
	FAQ Link	eBook p. 427 or CourseMate	

Competent Digital Citizen

Goal: I would like to be knowledgeable and well-informed about computers, mobile devices, and related technology, so that I am digitally literate in my personal and professional use of digital devices.

Topic	Resource	Location	Now you should . . .
System Software	Text	p. 398	Know the definition of system software
Start Up Process	Text/Figures	pp. 400–401	Be able to describe what occurs when you boot up a personal computer, and know the purpose of the registry
	Web Link	eBook p. 401 or CourseMate	
Command Language	Text	p. 403	Know the purpose of a command-line interface
Program Management	Text/Figures	pp. 404–405	Know various ways an operating system can handle programs
Virtual Memory	Text/Figure	p. 406	Know how a computer might use virtual memory
Spooling and Drivers	Text/Figure	pp. 407–408	Know how buffers and spooling work and the purpose of drivers
Eye Monitor	Looking Ahead	p. 409	Be familiar with a health-based performance monitor
	Link and Video	eBook p. 409 or CourseMate	
Operating Systems	Text/Figure	pp. 411–412	Know examples of operating systems in each category: stand-alone, server, and embedded
Windows History	Figure 8-15	p. 412	Be familiar with highlights of stand-alone Windows versions
Open vs. Closed Source	Ethics & Issues	p. 416	Be familiar with the issues around open and closed source programs
	Video	eBook p. 416 or CourseMate	
User Lockdown	Ethics & Issues	p. 418	Know how user lockdown relates to the smart phone industry
Computers in Education	Computer Usage @ Work	p. 429	Recognize how students and instructors use computers in school
	Link and Video	eBook p. 429 or CourseMate	
Touch Screens	Text	p. 430	Know how touch screens work
	Link and Video	eBook p. 430 or CourseMate	
Steve Wozniak	Text	p. 431	Be familiar with Steve Wozniak's impact on the computing industry
	Link and Video	eBook p. 431 or CourseMate	
Linus Torvalds	Text	p. 431	Be familiar with Linus Torvald's role with operating systems
	Link	eBook p. 431 or CourseMate	

Future Entrepreneur or Professional in a Digital Society

Goal: As I ponder my future, I envision myself as an entrepreneur or skilled professional using technology to support my business endeavors or job responsibilities. Along the way, I may interact with a variety of computer professionals — or I may just become one myself!

Topic	Resource	Location	Now you should . . .
Network Admin.	Text	p. 410	Know the role of a network administrator
Operating Systems	FAQ	p. 412	Know the market shares of various operating systems
	FAQ Link	eBook p. 412 or CourseMate	
Server Operating Systems	Text	pp. 417–418	Know the features of server operating systems: Windows Server, UNIX, Linus, Solaris, and NetWare
	Web Link	eBook p. 418 or CourseMate	
Systems Programmer	Exploring Computer Careers	CourseMate	Be familiar with the responsibilities and education required for a systems programmer

Preparing for a Test

Visit the Computer Concepts CourseMate at www.cengagebrain.com and then navigate to the Chapter 8 Web Apps resource for this book to prepare for your test.

Does your class use the Computer Concepts CourseMate Web site? If so, prepare for your test by using the Flash Cards, Study Guide, and Practice Test Web apps — available for your smart phone or tablet.

If your class does not use the Computer Concepts CourseMate Web site or you prefer to use your book, you can prepare for the test by doing the Quiz Yourself activities on pages 411, 421, and 429; reading the Chapter Review on pages 432–433; ensuring you know the definitions for the terms on page 434; and completing the Checkpoint exercises on pages 435–436. You also should know the material identified in the Chapter 8 Study Guide that follows.

Chapter 8 Study Guide

This study guide identifies material you should know for the Chapter 8 exam. You may want to write the answers in a notebook, enter them on your digital device, record them into a phone, or highlight them in your book. Choose whichever method helps you remember the best.

1. Define the term, system software. Identify the two types of system software.
2. Define operating system.
3. Define the terms, platform and cross-platform.
4. _____ is the process of starting or restarting a computer.
5. Differentiate a cold boot from a warm boot.
6. Define kernel.
7. Differentiate memory resident from nonresident.
8. Summarize the startup process on a personal computer.
9. Describe the purpose of the BIOS.
10. POST stands for _____.
11. Explain the purpose of the registry.
12. Differentiate between a boot drive and recovery disk.
13. Describe various shut down options: powering off, sleep mode, and hibernate.
14. Describe the purpose of a user interface. Differentiate between a GUI and command-line interface.
15. In relation to operating systems, explain the difference between single user/single tasking, single user/multitasking, preemptive multitasking, multiuser, and multiprocessing.
16. Differentiate between foreground and background.
17. Describe a fault-tolerant computer.
18. Describe how an operating system manages memory.
19. Describe virtual memory.
20. Define the term, thrashing. Identify ways to stop a computer from thrashing.
21. Explain how an operating system coordinates tasks or jobs.
22. Define the term, buffer. Explain how spooling uses buffers and a queue.
23. Define the term, driver. Explain how the operating system uses drivers and the role of Plug and Play.
24. Explain how properly to remove a USB flash drive.
25. Describe the purpose of a performance monitor.
26. _____ is a term that means computer error.

27. Briefly explain the types of updates that occur in an automatic update.

28. Describe a server operating system.

29. Describe the role of a network administrator. Differentiate administrator account from user account.

30. Define the terms, user name and password. Identify guidelines for selecting a good password.

31. Explain the reason for encryption.

32. Differentiate device-dependent from device-independent.

33. Differentiate among a stand-alone operating system, a server operating system, and an embedded operating system.

34. Summarize the features of these stand-alone operating systems: Windows, Mac OS, UNIX, and Linux.

35. State advantages of open source software.

36. Briefly describe various server operating systems: Windows Server, UNIX, Linux, Solaris, and NetWare.

37. Briefly describe and identify uses of Windows Embedded CE, Windows Phone, iPhone OS, BlackBerry, and Google Android.

38. Explain how it is possible to recover a deleted file.

39. Describe the purpose of a file manager, search utility, image viewer, uninstaller, and disk cleanup utility.

40. Describe the purpose of a disk defragmenter. Describe why a fragmented disk is slower than one that is defragmented.

41. Describe the purpose of a backup and restore utility, screen saver, and personal firewall.

42. Define computer virus and its relationship to malware. Identify signs of a virus infection. Describe the purpose of an antivirus program.

43. Describe the purpose of spyware and adware removers, Web filters, anti-spam programs, phishing filters, pop-up blockers, file compression utilities, media players, disc burning software, and personal computer maintenance utilities.

44. Explain the use of e-learning systems.

45. RIM's key product is its _____ smart phone.

46. _____ cofounded Apple with Steve Jobs.

47. Linus Torvalds created the open source operating system called _____.

48. Briefly describe some considerations when purchasing a desktop computer, notebook computer, smart phone, portable media player, and digital camera.

Check This Out

As technology changes, you must keep up with updates, new products, breakthroughs, and recent advances to remain digitally literate. The list below identifies topics related to this chapter that you should explore to keep current. In parentheses beside each topic, you will find a search term to help begin your research using a search engine, such as Google.

1. **largest operating system market share** (search for: top market share operating systems)

2. **features of latest Windows operating system** (search for: latest Microsoft Windows features)

3. **features of newest Apple OS operating system** (search for: latest Macintosh OS features)

4. **recent UNIX operating system elements** (search for: new UNIX features)

5. **new Linux GUI enhancements** (search for: Linux GUI)

6. **latest Windows Server edition** (search for: recent Windows Server)

7. **recent Windows Phone operating system** (search for: latest Windows mobile OS)

8. **new iPhone and iPad OS features** (search for: iOS news)

9. **popular utility software** (search for: best utility programs)

10. **best utilities to back up data** (search for: backup utilities review)

11. **top antivirus programs** (search for: popular antivirus software)

12. **widely used spyware removal programs** (search for: popular spyware programs)

13. **popular e-learning management systems** (search for: top e-learning software)

14. **updates about Steve Wozniak's projects** (search for: Steve Wozniak news)

15. **latest guidelines for purchasing computers** (search for: computer buying guide)

For current news and information
Check us out on Facebook and Twitter. See your instructor or the Computer Concepts CourseMate for specific information.

Communications and Networks

Chapter 9

Why Should I Learn About Communications and Networks?

"I use my new smart phone to send text messages, send and receive voice mail, and navigate using a GPS app. At home, I have a broadband Internet connection, and I also access the Internet wirelessly at local hot spots or anywhere on campus. What more do I need to learn about communications and networks?"

True, you may be familiar with some of the material in this chapter, but do you know . . .

"What more do I need to learn about communications and networks?"

- How to determine hot spot locations throughout the country? (p. 480, FAQ)
- How tolls are collected automatically at tollbooths using a RFID reader? (p. 481, RFID)
- How you are able to access your school network wirelessly? (p. 487, Wireless Access Points)
- Why your Internet access provider may not be stating accurate connection speeds? (p. 492, Ethics & Issues)
- How the agriculture industry uses computers to help grow crops? (p. 497, Computer Usage @ Work)
- Which communications company's name is derived from the Roman goddess of truth? (p. 499, Companies on the Cutting Edge)
- How to set up and install a Wi-Fi home network? (p. 508–509 and Computer Concepts CourseMate, Learn How To)
- How to view Windows Firewall security settings? (Windows Exercises, Computer Concepts CourseMate)

For these answers and to discover much more information essential to this course, read Chapter 9 and visit the associated Computer Concepts CourseMate at www.cengagebrain.com.

Customize Your Learning Experience

Q & A How can I meet one or more of these goals?

Make use of the goal's resources for each chapter in the book and you should meet that goal by the end of the course.

Adapt this book to meet your needs by determining your goal. Would you like to be an informed digital consumer? A productive technology user? A safe user, protected from the risks in a digital world? A competent digital citizen? A future entrepreneur or professional in a digital society?

Every chapter in this Student Success Guide identifies resources targeted toward each of these goals, along with criteria to verify you understand the resources' content. Resources may be located in the textbook, on the Computer Concepts CourseMate Web site, in the interactive eBook, and on the Web.

Informed Digital Consumer

Goal: I would like to understand the terminology used in Web or print advertisements that sell computers, mobile devices, and related technology, as well as the jargon used by sales associates in computer or electronics stores, so that I can make informed purchasing decisions.

Topic	Resource	Location	Now you should . . .
Internet Connections	Text/Figure	pp. 483–484	Be aware of costs and transfer rates of various Internet connections
	Drag and Drop Figure 9-24	eBook p. 483 or CourseMate	
Modems	Text/Figures and FAQ	pp. 485–487	Know the purpose and uses of various modem types: dial-up modems, digital modems (ISDN, DSL, and cable), and wireless modems
	Web Links	eBook p. 486 or CourseMate	
	FAQ Link	eBook p. 486, or Cable Internet Service link, CourseMate	

Continued on next page

Continued from previous page

Topic	Resource	Location	Now you should . . .
Network Cards	Text/Figure	p. 487	Know the purpose and styles of network cards
Wireless Access Point	Text/Figure	p. 487	Know the purpose of a wireless access point
Routers	Text/Figure and FAQ	p. 488	Know the purpose of routers
	Web Link	eBook p. 488 or CourseMate	Be familiar with the features and costs of wireless routers
Mobile TV	Links and Video	eBook p. 495 or CourseMate	Be familiar with how to watch live programs on a computer or mobile device
	Innovative Computing	p. 495	
	Video	At the Movies, CourseMate	
Verizon	Text	p. 499	Be familiar with Verizon's products and services
	Link	eBook p. 499 or CourseMate	

Productive Technology User

Goal: I would like to learn ways that technology can benefit me at home, work, and school. I also would like to learn helpful techniques for using technology so that I can perform tasks more efficiently and be more productive in daily activities.

Topic	Resource	Location	Now you should . . .
Uses of Computer Communications	Text/Figure	pp. 461–462	Know the uses of computer communications previously discussed
	Drag and Drop Figure 9-2	eBook p. 462 or CourseMate	
	Web Link		
Wireless Messaging	Text/Figure and FAQ	pp. 462–464	Know the guidelines and uses of text, picture/video, and wireless instant messaging
	Figure Video	eBook p. 463 or CourseMate	
	FAQ and Web Link		
Wireless Internet Access Points	Text/Figure	pp. 464–465	Be familiar with hot spots and mobile wireless networks
Cybercafés	Text/Figure	p. 466	Know the services offered by cybercafés
GPS	Text/Figure	pp. 466–467	Know how GPS works, and name devices with GPS capability
	Web Link	eBook p. 466 or CourseMate	
Voice Mail	Text	p. 467	Know how voice mail and visual voice mail work
Internet Peer-to-Peer	Text/Figure	p. 475	Know the uses of a file sharing or P2P network
	Web Link	eBook p. 475 or CourseMate	
Wi-Fi	Text/Figure and FAQ	pp. 479–480	Know 802.11 series standards and transfer rates and uses of Wi-Fi and hot spots
	Drag and Drop Figure 9-20	eBook p. 479 or CourseMate	
	FAQ Link	eBook p. 480, or Hot Spots link, CourseMate	

Continued on next page

Continued from previous page

Topic	Resource	Location	Now you should . . .
Bluetooth, UWB, IrDA	Text	pp. 480–481	Know some uses of Bluetooth, UWB, and IrDA communications
Communications Software	Text	p. 482	Know the purpose of communications software
Internet Connections	Text/Figures	pp. 482–485	Know how these Internet connections work: dial-up, ISDN, DSL, FTTP, T-carrier, and ATM
	Web Link	eBook p. 484 or CourseMate	
Home Networks	Text/Figure	pp. 489–490	Know benefits of a home network, the types of wired and wireless home networks, and how to set up a home network
	Web Link	eBook p. 489 or CourseMate	
	Figure 9-33 Animation		
	Learn How To	pp. 508–509 and CourseMate	
Modems and Network Connections	Windows Exercises	CourseMate	Know how to use Windows to learn about the modem connected to a computer and view the computer's network connections
Gmail	Web Apps	CourseMate	Know how to use Gmail to send and receive e-mail messages

Safe User, Protected from the Risks in a Digital World

Goal: I would like to take measures to (1) protect my computers, devices, and data from loss, damage, or misuse; (2) minimize or prevent risks associated with using technology; and (3) minimize the environmental impact of using computers and related devices.

Topic	Resource	Location	Now you should . . .
IP Addresses	FAQ	p. 478	Know if an IP address can be used to determine a device's location and recover stolen computers
	FAQ Video	eBook p. 478 or CourseMate	
Unsecured Networks	Ethics & Issues	p. 480	Know some issues associated with unsecured wireless networks
Internet Connection Speeds	Ethics & Issues	p. 492	Know that advertised connection speeds may differ from actual speeds
Cellular and Wi-Fi Radiation	Ethics & Issues	p. 494	Know about potential health effects from cell phones, cellular antennas, and Wi-Fi devices
Wireless Security	Labs	CourseMate	Be familiar with ways to secure an access point
Windows Firewall	Windows Exercises	CourseMate	Be familiar with how to use Windows Firewall

Competent Digital Citizen

Goal: I would like to be knowledgeable and well-informed about computers, mobile devices, and related technology, so that I am digitally literate in my personal and professional use of digital devices.

Topic	Resource	Location	Now you should . . .
Communications	Text/Figure	pp. 460–461	Know the components required in a communications system
Print Media	Ethics & Issues	p. 465	Be aware of the impact of high-speed broadband on print media
	Video	eBook p. 465 or CourseMate	
Geocaching	Innovative Computing	p. 466	Be familiar with how geocaching uses GPS technology
	Link and Video	eBook p. 466 or CourseMate	

Continued on next page

Continued from previous page

Topic	Resource	Location	Now you should . . .
Body Area Network	Looking Ahead	p. 471	Be familiar with the uses of body area networks
	Link and Video	eBook p. 471 or CourseMate	
LANs, MANs, WANs	Text/Figures	pp. 471–473	Know the differences among LANs, MANs, and WANs
	Labs	CourseMate	
Internet Usage	Ethics & Issues	p. 474	Be familiar with issues surrounding Internet usage controls
IP Addresses	FAQ Link	eBook p. 478, or IP Addresses link, CourseMate	Know how IP addresses work
WAP	Text/Figure	p. 482	Know the uses of WAP
Communications Channel	Text/Figure	pp. 491–492	Know the meaning of bandwidth and latency, and the types of transmission media used on a communications channel
Physical Transmission Media	Text/Figures	pp. 492–493	Be familiar with transfer rates and composition of twisted-pair cable, coaxial cable, and fiber-optic cable
	Drag and Drop Figures 9-35, 9-37, and 9-38	eBook pp. 492–493 or CourseMate	
Wireless Transmission Media	Text/Figures	pp. 494–496	Be familiar with transfer rates of and technologies used in infrared, broadcast radio, cellular radio, microwaves, and communications satellite
	Drag and Drop Figure 9-39	eBook p. 494 or CourseMate	
Computers in Agriculture	Computer Usage @ Work	p. 497	Recognize how computers are used in the agriculture industry
	Link and Video	eBook p. 497 or CourseMate	
Network Communications	Text	p. 498	Recognize that data in a network flows through several layers
	Link and Video	eBook p. 498 or CourseMate	
Cisco	Text	p. 499	Be familiar with Cisco's products and services
	Link and Video	eBook p. 499 or CourseMate	
Robert Metcalf	Text	p. 499	Be familiar with Robert Metcalf's impact on network communications
	Link	eBook p. 499 or CourseMate	

Future Entrepreneur or Professional in a Digital Society

Goal: As I ponder my future, I envision myself as an entrepreneur or skilled professional using technology to support my business endeavors or job responsibilities. Along the way, I may interact with a variety of computer professionals — or I may just become one myself!

Topic	Resource	Location	Now you should . . .
Groupware	Text	p. 467	Be familiar with the benefits of groupware in business
Collaboration	Text/Figure	p. 468	Be familiar with collaboration tools: collaborative software, reviewing via e-mail, and document management systems
	Web Link	eBook p. 468 or CourseMate	
Web Services	Text/Figure	p. 469	Know the purpose of Web services in business
Network Advantages	Text/Figure	pp. 470–471	Know the reasons businesses use networks
Network Architectures	Text/Figures	pp. 473–474	Know the difference between client/server and peer-to-peer networks

Continued on next page

Continued from previous page

Topic	Resource	Location	Now you should . . .
Network Topologies	Text/Figures	pp. 475–477	Know the differences among star, bus, and ring networks
Intranets	Text	p. 477	Know how businesses use Intranets and extranets
Ethernet, Token Ring, TCP/IP	Text	pp. 477–478	Be able to differentiate among the Ethernet, token ring, and TCP/IP network communications standards
RFID	Text/Figure	p. 481	Know how RFID works and its uses
	Web Link	eBook p. 481 or CourseMate	
WiMAX	Text	p. 482	Know the purpose, types, and uses of WiMAX
Hubs and Switches	Text/Figure	pp. 488–489	Know the purpose of hubs and switches
Network Specialist	Exploring Computer Careers	CourseMate	Be familiar with the responsibilities and education required for a network specialist

Preparing for a Test

Visit the Computer Concepts CourseMate at www.cengagebrain.com and then navigate to the Chapter 9 Web Apps resource for this book to prepare for your test.

Does your class use the Computer Concepts CourseMate Web site? If so, prepare for your test by using the Flash Cards, Study Guide, and Practice Test Web apps — available for your smart phone or tablet.

If your class does not use the Computer Concepts CourseMate Web site or you prefer to use your book, you can prepare for the test by doing the Quiz Yourself activities on pages 469, 485, and 497; reading the Chapter Review on pages 500–501; ensuring you know the definitions for the terms on page 502; and completing the Checkpoint exercises on pages 503–504. You also should know the material identified in the Chapter 9 Study Guide that follows.

Chapter 9 Study Guide

This study guide identifies material you should know for the Chapter 9 exam. You may want to write the answers in a notebook, enter them on your digital device, record them into a phone, or highlight them in your book. Choose whichever method helps you remember the best.

1. Define computer communications.

2. Discuss the purpose of the components required for successful communications: sending device, communications device, communications channel, and receiving device.

3. Identify various sending and receiving devices.

4. Briefly describe these communications: blogs, chat rooms, e-mail, fax, FTP, instant messaging, Internet, RSS, video conferencing, VoIP, Web, Web 2.0, and wikis.

5. A synonym for text messaging is _____.

6. Describe text messaging. Identify a use of a CSC (common short code).

7. Describe picture messaging and video messaging.

8. A synonym for picture/video messaging is _____.

9. Define wireless Internet access point.

10. Define hot spot. Describe three hot spot technologies.

11. Describe a mobile wireless network.

12. Describe a cybercafé.

13. GPS stands for _____. Give examples of GPS receivers. Cite uses of GPS technology.

14. Explain geocaching.

15. Describe uses of these computer communications: groupware, collaboration, voice mail, and Web services.

16. Define the term, network. List advantages of using a network.

17. EFT stands for _____.

18. Differentiate among LANs, MANs, and WANs.

19. Describe how sensors might work in a body area network (BAN). Identify potential uses of BANs.

20. A server sometimes is called a(n) _____ computer. State examples of dedicated servers.

21. Differentiate between client/server and peer-to-peer networks.

22. Describe how a P2P network works.

Continued on next page

Continued from previous page

23. Differentiate among a star network, bus network, and ring network.

24. Describe how an intranet works. Identify the relationship of an extranet to an intranet.

25. Describe the purpose of network standards and protocols.

26. Differentiate among the Ethernet, token ring, and TCP/IP standards.

27. Describe the Wi-Fi standard. Identify its distance limitations. Name some uses of Wi-Fi.

28. Describe the Bluetooth standard. Identify its distance limitations. Give examples of some Bluetooth devices.

29. Describe UWB and IrDA standards.

30. RFID stands for _____. Explain how RFID works.

31. Describe the WiMAX standard.

32. Explain the purpose of communications software.

33. Describe various types of lines for communications over the telephone network: dial-up, ISDN, DSL, FTTP, T-carrier, and ATM.

34. Differentiate a dial-up modem from a digital modem. Explain differences between ISDN modems, DSL modems, and cable modems.

35. Describe the purpose of wireless modems and network cards. Identify types of each.

36. State the purpose of a wireless access point and a router. Explain security features built into some routers. Identify the best location for a router.

37. Define the purpose of a hub and/or switch.

38. Describe the advantages of a home network. Discuss different wired and wireless ways to set up a home network.

39. Define the terms, bandwidth and latency.

40. Describe the purpose of transmission media. Define the term, broadband media.

41. Explain why advertised Internet connections speeds may differ from actual speeds.

42. Define noise, as it relates to computer communications.

43. Describe characteristics of these physical transmission media: twisted-pair cable, coaxial cable, and fiber-optic cable.

44. Describe characteristics of these wireless transmission media: infrared, broadcast radio, cellular radio, microwaves, and communications satellite.

45. Describe the purpose of the OSI reference model.

46. Cisco manufactures _____ equipment.

47. Identify services by Verizon.

48. Robert Metcalfe coinvented the _____ standard for computer communications.

Check This Out

As technology changes, you must keep up with updates, new products, breakthroughs, and recent advances to remain digitally literate. The list below identifies topics related to this chapter that you should explore to keep current. In parentheses beside each topic, you will find a search term to help begin your research using a search engine, such as Google.

1. news of using a cell phone as a primary telephone (search for: cell phone primary phone)

2. latest developments of working securely from a hot spot (search for: wireless security hot spot)

3. recent company use of GPS applications for tracking (search for: GPS tracking system)

4. recent geocaching developments (search for: new geocaching adventures)

5. popular online groupware applications (search for: best groupware reviews)

6. new document management systems for collaboration (search for: electronic document management software)

7. widely used mashups (search for: best mashups)

8. latest electronic funds transfers using cell phones (search for: cell phone transfer funds news)

9. popular wireless LAN devices (search for: best wireless LAN hardware)

10. recent software to monitor Internet use (search for: Internet usage control)

11. widely used network communications standards (search for: network communications standards reviews)

12. Wi-Fi Internet access developments (search for: new Wi-Fi Internet technology)

13. popular Bluetooth products (search for: top Bluetooth devices)

14. latest digital modems (search for: digital modem news)

15. useful advice for creating a wireless home network (search for: wireless home network guide)

For current news and information
Check us out on Facebook and Twitter. See your instructor or the Computer Concepts CourseMate for specific information.

Database Management

Why Should I Learn About Database Management?

"I realize my school maintains data about me on its computer system, including my contact information, schedule, and grades. At home, I use my computer to keep track of my income and expenses. I also have a list of repairs and modifications I have made to the car I am restoring. So, why do I need to learn about managing databases?"

True, you may be familiar with some of the material in this chapter, but do you know . . .

"Why do I need to learn about managing databases?"

- Why your privacy may be compromised when your personal data is stored in Internet databases? (p. 516, Ethics & Issues)
- How to verify the accuracy of your credit report? (p. 517, FAQ)
- What action you should take if you accidentally discover a file with private data on a publically accessible area of the Internet? (p. 531, Ethics & Issues)
- How a GIS works? (p. 534, Object-Oriented Databases)
- How databases automate processes in the health care industry? (p. 539, Computer Usage @ Work)
- Who developed the relational database design structure that is used for most databases used today? (p. 541, Technology Trailblazers)
- How to organize files using folders? (p. 550 and Computer Concepts CourseMate, Learn How To)
- How to manage folders on a storage device? (Windows Exercises, Computer Concepts CourseMate)

For these answers and to discover much more information essential to this course, read Chapter 10 and visit the associated Computer Concepts CourseMate at www.cengagebrain.com.

Customize Your Learning Experience

Q & A

How can I meet one or more of these goals?

Make use of the goal's resources for each chapter in the book and you should meet that goal by the end of the course.

Adapt this book to meet your needs by determining your goal. Would you like to be an informed digital consumer? A productive technology user? A safe user, protected from the risks in a digital world? A competent digital citizen? A future entrepreneur or professional in a digital society?

Every chapter in this Student Success Guide identifies resources targeted toward each of these goals, along with criteria to verify you understand the resources' content. Resources may be located in the textbook, on the Computer Concepts CourseMate Web site, in the interactive eBook, and on the Web.

Informed Digital Consumer

Goal: I would like to understand the terminology used in Web or print advertisements that sell computers, mobile devices, and related technology, as well as the jargon used by sales associates in computer or electronics stores, so that I can make informed purchasing decisions.

Topic	Resource	Location	Now you should . . .
DBMSs	Figure	p. 527	Know the popular DBMSs
	Web Link	eBook p. 527 or CourseMate	
Database Vendors	FAQ	p. 527	Know the market share of database vendors
Data Models and Terminology	Text/Figures	p. 533	Know the various data models and data terminology used in file processing and relational database environments
	Drag and Drop Figure 10-19	eBook p. 533 or CourseMate	

Productive Technology User

Goal: I would like to learn ways that technology can benefit me at home, work, and school. I also would like to learn helpful techniques for using technology so that I can perform tasks more efficiently and be more productive in daily activities.

Topic	Resource	Location	Now you should . . .
Information	Text	pp. 516–517	Know the qualities of valuable information for decision making
Database vs. Spreadsheets	FAQ	p. 519	Know when to use a database versus a spreadsheet
	FAQ Link	eBook p. 519, or Databases and Spreadsheets link, CourseMate	
Adding Records	Text/Figure	p. 520	Be familiar with reasons for and process of adding records to a file
Modifying Records	Text/Figure	p. 521	Be familiar with reasons for and process of modifying records in a file
Deleting Records	Text/Figure	p. 522	Be familiar with reasons for and process of deleting records in a file
Data Dictionary	Text/Figure	pp. 527–528	Be familiar with the use of a data dictionary
	Drag and Drop Figure 10-12	eBook p. 528 or CourseMate	
File Retrieval and Maintenance	Text/Figures	pp. 528–531	Be familiar with the use of query languages, query by example, forms, and report generators
	Drag and Drop Figure 10-13	eBook p. 529 or CourseMate	
SQL	Text/Figure	p. 534	Be familiar with SQL
	Link and Video	eBook p. 534 or CourseMate	
Employee as a User	Text/Figure	p. 538	Know how employees uses databases
Photo Sharing Site	Video	At the Movies, CourseMate	Know how a photo sharing site keeps its data
Spreadsheets	Labs	CourseMate	Be familiar with advanced uses of spreadsheets
Databases	Labs	CourseMate	Be familiar with advanced uses of databases
Files and Folders	Learn How To	pp. 550–551 and CourseMate	Know how to use Windows to organize, manage, and search for files and folders
	Windows Exercises		
Calendar	Web Apps	CourseMate	Know how to use Windows Live Calendar

Safe User, Protected from the Risks in a Digital World

Goal: I would like to take measures to (1) protect my computers, devices, and data from loss, damage, or misuse; (2) minimize or prevent risks associated with using technology; and (3) minimize the environmental impact of using computers and related devices.

Topic	Resource	Location	Now you should . . .
Privacy	Ethics & Issues	p. 516	Realize privacy issues associated with Internet databases
Credit Report	FAQ	p. 517	Know how to check the accuracy of your credit report
	Link and Video	eBook p. 517 or CourseMate	
Government Data	Ethics & Issues	p. 519	Know the type of data the government stores about citizens and foreigners who travel to the United States
Criminal Databases	Ethics & Issues	p. 526	Know issues related to criminal databases
Data Security	Text	p. 531	Be familiar with levels of access privileges
Backup and Recovery	Text/Figure	pp. 531–532	Know the purpose of a backup, a log, a recovery utility, and continuous backup
Security Breaches	Ethics & Issues	p. 537	Know the privacy issues surrounding database security
	Video	eBook p. 537 or CourseMate	

Competent Digital Citizen

Goal: I would like to be knowledgeable and well-informed about computers, mobile devices, and related technology, so that I am digitally literate in my personal and professional use of digital devices.

Topic	Resource	Location	Now you should . . .
Databases	Text/Figure	pp. 514–516	Know the purpose of a database and database software, and how database software is used to process data into information
	Figure 10-1 Animation	eBook p. 514 or CourseMate	
Data Integrity	Text	p. 516	Understand the importance of data integrity
Hierarchy of Data	Text/Figures	pp. 517–519	Know the difference between characters, fields, records, and files; know data types of fields
	Drag and Drop Figure 10-2	p. 517	
Baseball Databases	Innovative Computing	p. 523	Know how databases are used in baseball memorabilia authentication and online baseball games
	Link and Video	eBook p. 523 or CourseMate	
Voter Databases	Innovative Computing	p. 530	Be familiar with how political campaigners use voter databases
Relational Databases	Text/Figure	pp. 533–534	Know the organization and uses of relational databases
Object-Oriented Databases	Text/Figure	pp. 534–535	Know the organization and uses of object-oriented databases
GIS Databases	FAQ	p. 535	Know about geographic information system databases
	FAQ Link	eBook p. 535, or GIS Databases link, CourseMate	
	Figure Video		
Multidimensional Databases	Text	p. 535	Know the organization and uses of multidimensional databases
Web Databases	Text/Figure	pp. 536–537	Be familiar with the uses and operation of Web databases
Portable Media Player	FAQ	p. 537	Know how portable media players use databases
	FAQ Link	eBook p. 537, or Media Player Databases link, CourseMate	
DNA Barcoding	Looking Ahead	p. 538	Be familiar with how databases are used to catalog species of plants, animals, and microbes
	Link and Video	eBook p. 538 or CourseMate	
Normalization	Text/Figure	p. 540	Know how databases are normalized
	Link and Video	eBook p. 540 or CourseMate	
E. F. Codd	Text	p. 541	Be familiar with E. F. Codd's impact on relational databases
	Link	eBook p. 541 or CourseMate	
Larry Ellison	Text	p. 541	Be familiar with Larry Ellison's impact on relational databases
	Link and Video	eBook p. 541 or CourseMate	

Future Entrepreneur or Professional in a Digital Society

Goal: As I ponder my future, I envision myself as an entrepreneur or skilled professional using technology to support my business endeavors or job responsibilities. Along the way, I may interact with a variety of computer professionals — or I may just become one myself!

Topic	Resource	Location	Now you should . . .
Data Validation	Text/Figure	pp. 522–524	Know the various checks programmers use to validate data
	Web Link	eBook p. 523 or CourseMate	
File Processing System	Text	p. 524	Be familiar with how organizations use file processing systems and potential disadvantages
Database Approach	Text and FAQ	p. 524-526	Be familiar with how organizations use a database approach and potential benefits over file processing systems
	Drag and Drop Figure 10-10	eBook p. 525 or CourseMate	
E-Forms	Web Link	eBook p. 530 or CourseMate	Know how to use e-forms for surveys and database connectivity
Data Warehouses	Text	p. 536	Know how organizations use data warehouses
Database Design Guidelines	Text	pp. 537–538	Be familiar with guidelines for database design
	Web Link	eBook p. 537 or CourseMate	
Database Analysts and Administrators	Text	p. 538	Know the role of database analysts and administrators, and be familiar with responsibilities and education required for database administrators
	Web Link	eBook p. 538 or CourseMate	
	Exploring Computer Careers	CourseMate	
Health Sciences	Computer Usage @ Work	p. 539	Know how professionals in the health sciences field use computers to support their activities
	Link and Video	eBook p. 539 or CourseMate	
Oracle	Text	p. 541	Be familiar with Oracle's enterprise products and services
	Link	eBook p. 541 or CourseMate	
Sybase	Text	p. 541	Be familiar with Sybase's enterprise products and services
	Link	eBook p. 541 or CourseMate	

Preparing for a Test

Visit the Computer Concepts CourseMate at **www.cengagebrain.com** and then navigate to the Chapter 10 Web Apps resource for this book to prepare for your test.

Does your class use the Computer Concepts CourseMate Web site? If so, prepare for your test by using the Flash Cards, Study Guide, and Practice Test Web apps — available for your smart phone or tablet.

If your class does not use the Computer Concepts CourseMate Web site or you prefer to use your book, you can prepare for the test by doing the Quiz Yourself activities on pages 524, 532, and 539; reading the Chapter Review on pages 542–543; ensuring you know the definitions for the terms on page 544; and completing the Checkpoint exercises on pages 545–546. You also should know the material identified in the Chapter 10 Study Guide that follows.

Chapter 10 Study Guide

This study guide identifies material you should know for the Chapter 10 exam. You may want to write the answers in a notebook, enter them on your digital device, record them into a phone, or highlight them in your book. Choose whichever method helps you remember the best.

1. Define database. Explain the purpose of a database management system (DBMS).

2. Explain the meaning of data integrity.

3. GIGO stands for _____. Describe the meaning of this term.

4. Describe seven qualities of valuable information.

5. Identify ways to verify the accuracy of your credit report.

6. Order these terms from smallest to largest: records, characters, files, fields. Define and give an example for each term.

7. Identify common data types.

8. Define file maintenance.

9. Identify reasons these activities are performed: adding records to a file, modifying records in a file, and deleting records from a file.

10. Describe ways DBMSs manage deleted records.

11. Explain the purpose of validation.

12. Describe and give an example of each of these types of validity checks: alphabetic, numeric, range, consistency, completeness, and check digit.

13. Explain how a file processing system works. Identify two weaknesses of a file processing system.

14. Explain how the database approach works. Identify five strengths of the database approach. Identify some disadvantages of the database approach.

15. Differentiate a front-end program from a back-end program.

16. Explain the significance of Megan's Law.

17. Explain why a database cannot completely eliminate redundant data.

18. Identify the database vendors with the largest market share.

19. Another term for data dictionary is _____.

20. Identify the types of details stored in a data dictionary.

21. Define the term, default value. Give an example.

22. Define the term, query.

23. Describe the purpose of these file retrieval and maintenance tools: query language, query by example (QBE), form, and report generator.

24. Identify the purpose of a wizard.

25. Describe how political campaigners can use databases.

26. Explain how e-forms can work with databases.

27. Define access privileges. Identify various levels of access privileges. Explain the intent of the principle of least privilege.

28. Describe how a DBMS uses backups.

29. Define the use and contents of a log.

30. Define how a DBMS uses recovery utilities. Differentiate between a rollforward and a rollback.

31. Describe advantages and disadvantages of continuous backup.

32. Define data model. Name examples.

33. A user of a relational database refers to a file as a(n) _____, a record as a(n) _____, and a field as a(n) _____.

34. A developer of a relational database refers to a file as a(n) _____, a record as a(n) _____, and a field as a(n) _____.

35. Describe the organization of relational databases. Define the terms, relationship and normalization.

36. SQL stands for _____.

37. Differentiate between SQL and OQL.

Continued on next page

Continued from previous page

38. Describe the organization of object-oriented databases. Give examples of applications that use object-oriented databases.

39. Describe the organization of multidimensional databases.

40. Explain the purpose of data warehouses and the reason they use data mining.

41. Give examples of databases on the Web.

42. Explain the purpose of a CGI script.

43. Identify guidelines for designing a database.

44. Differentiate between a database analyst and a database administrator.

45. Identify ways computers and databases are used in the health sciences field.

46. Briefly describe the normalization process.

47. Larry Ellison founded _____.

Check This Out

As technology changes, you must keep up with updates, new products, breakthroughs, and recent advances to remain digitally literate. The list below identifies topics related to this chapter that you should explore to keep current. In parentheses beside each topic, you will find a search term to help begin your research using a search engine, such as Google.

1. **widely used databases in education** (search for: popular databases education)

2. **recent government dragnets used to fight crime** (search for: latest government dragnets)

3. **popular data validation techniques** (search for: latest data validation checks)

4. **updates about database management systems** (search for: recent database management systems features)

5. **largest database management systems market share** (search for: top market share database management systems)

6. **recent data security breaches** (search for: security breaches news)

7. **popular database backup and recovery techniques** (search for: latest database backup recovery)

8. **new relational database software** (search for: relational database news)

9. **popular business object-oriented databases** (search for: objected-oriented database business)

10. **recent uses of multidimensional databases** (search for: multidimensional database examples)

11. **new GIS databases available from the U.S. Geological Survey** (search for: USGS Global GIS)

12. **widely used Web databases** (search for: popular Web databases)

13. **updates about database administrator jobs** (search for: database administrator duties)

14. **developments of identifying species using DNA barcoding** (search for: DNA barcoding news)

15. **updates about Oracle's social network applications** (search for: Oracle Public Cloud)

For current news and information
Check us out on Facebook and Twitter. See your instructor or the Computer Concepts CourseMate for specific information.

Chapter 11 — Computer Security and Safety, Ethics, and Privacy

Why Should I Learn About Computer Security and Safety, Ethics, and Privacy?

"I am careful when browsing the Internet and never open e-mail messages from unknown senders. No one would guess that I use my dog's name as my password on home and school networks. I use a surge protector and an ENERGY STAR monitor. What more do I need to know about security, ethics, and privacy while using a computer or mobile device?"

True, you may be familiar with some of the material in this chapter, but do you know . . .

"What more do I need to know about security, ethics, and privacy while using a computer or mobile device?"

- Which popular online services may protect your computer from Internet security breaches? (p. 558, Internet and Network Attacks)
- How to prevent tendonitis, eye strain, and other injuries? (p. 579, Computers and Health Risks)
- Which merchants analyze your conversations and shopping habits? (p. 585, Innovative Computing)
- How computers monitor and maintain national and local security? (p. 591, Computer Usage @ Work)
- Who is one of the world's leading computer security experts? (p. 593, Technology Trailblazers)
- How to back up files on an offsite Internet server? (p. 602 and Computer Concepts CourseMate, Learn How To)
- How to receive system updates automatically? (Windows Exercises, Computer Concepts CourseMate)
- How law enforcement officials investigate evidence found on computers and digital devices? (pp. 606–616, Digital Forensics Special Feature)

For these answers and to discover much more information essential to this course, read Chapter 11 and visit the associated Computer Concepts CourseMate at www.cengagebrain.com.

Customize Your Learning Experience

Q & A — How can I meet one or more of these goals?

Make use of the goal's resources for each chapter in the book and you should meet that goal by the end of the course.

Adapt this book to meet your needs by determining your goal. Would you like to be an informed digital consumer? A productive technology user? A safe user, protected from the risks in a digital world? A competent digital citizen? A future entrepreneur or professional in a digital society?

Every chapter in this Student Success Guide identifies resources targeted toward each of these goals, along with criteria to verify you understand the resources' content. Resources may be located in the textbook, on the Computer Concepts CourseMate Web site, in the interactive eBook, and on the Web.

Informed Digital Consumer

Goal: I would like to understand the terminology used in Web or print advertisements that sell computers, mobile devices, and related technology, as well as the jargon used by sales associates in computer or electronics stores, so that I can make informed purchasing decisions.

Topic	Resource	Location	Now you should . . .
Antivirus Programs	Text/Figure	p. 560	Be familiar with names of popular antivirus programs
Firewall Software	Text/Figure	p. 564	Be familiar with names of personal firewall software
McAfee	Text	p. 593	Be familiar with McAfee's products and services
	Link	eBook p. 593 or CourseMate	
Symantec	Text	p. 593	Be familiar with Symantec's products and services
	Link	eBook p. 593 or CourseMate	

Productive Technology User

Goal: I would like to learn ways that technology can benefit me at home, work, and school. I also would like to learn helpful techniques for using technology so that I can perform tasks more efficiently and be more productive in daily activities.

Topic	Resource	Location	Now you should . . .
License Agreement	Text/Figure	pp. 571–572	Know what is allowed and not allowed with a software license
Wireless Network	FAQ Link	eBook p. 578 or CourseMate	Know how to set up a home wireless network
Computer Ethics	Text/Figure	p. 581	Be aware of ethical/unethical computer uses
	Labs	CourseMate	
Code of Conduct	Text/Figure	pp. 582–583	Be familiar with the IT code of conduct
Cookies	Text/Figure	pp. 585–587	Know the uses of cookies, how they work, how to view accepted cookies, and how to adjust cookie settings
	Web Link	eBook p. 586 or CourseMate	
	Labs	CourseMate	
Privacy Laws	Text/Figure	pp. 588–589	Be familiar with the intent of various privacy laws
Windows Media Player	Windows Exercises	CourseMate	Know how to use Windows Media Player to play a CD
Windows Updates	Windows Exercises	CourseMate	Know how to use Windows Update
Offsite Backup	Learn How To	p. 602 and CourseMate	Know how to back up files to an offsite Internet server
Windows Firewall	Learn How To	p. 603 and CourseMate	Know how to use Windows Firewall
Dictionary	Web Apps	CourseMate	Know how to use Dictionary.com

Safe User, Protected from the Risks in a Digital World

Goal: I would like to take measures to (1) protect my computers, devices, and data from loss, damage, or misuse; (2) minimize or prevent risks associated with using technology; and (3) minimize the environmental impact of using computers and related devices.

Topic	Resource	Location	Now you should . . .
Online Security	Text/Figure	p. 558	Be familiar with popular online security services
CERT/CC	Text	p. 558	Know the role of the Computer Emergency Response Team Coordination Center
	Web Link	eBook p. 558 or CourseMate	
Viruses and Other Malware	Text/Figures	pp. 560–561	Know ways to protect computers and devices from viruses and other malware
	Videos	eBook p. 561 or CourseMate, and At the Movies, CourseMate	
Botnets	FAQ Link and Video	eBook p. 562 or CourseMate	Know how to protect a computer from botnets
Firewalls	Text/Figures	pp. 563–564	Know how firewalls protect network resources
Unauthorized Access	Text/Figure	p. 565	Know how to protect your computer from unauthorized intrusions
Passwords	Text/Figure/FAQ	pp. 566–567	Know how to select a good password and protect it
PINs	Text	p. 568	Know the uses of PINs and why you should select them carefully
Biometrics and Privacy	Ethics & Issues	p. 568	Be aware of privacy issues surrounding use of biometric devices
	Video	eBook p. 568 or CourseMate	
Identity Theft	FAQ Link	eBook p. 569 or CourseMate	Know ways to protect yourself from identity theft

Continued on next page

Continued from previous page

Topic	Resource	Location	Now you should . . .
Hardware Theft	Text/Figure	p. 570	Be aware of ways to protect against hardware theft
Surge Protectors	Text/Figures/FAQ	pp. 576–677	Know the purpose of surge protectors and how they work
	Web Link	eBook p. 576 or CourseMate	
Wireless Security	Text and FAQ	pp. 578–579	Be familiar with ways to improve the security of wireless networks
Health Risks	Text/Figures	pp. 579–580	Know how to protect yourself from RSIs and CVS, how to design an ergonomic work area, and recognize computer addiction
Information Accuracy	Text/Figure	p. 582	Recognize that not all information is accurate
Green Computing	Text/Figure	pp. 583–584	Know strategies that support green computing
Information Privacy	Text/Figure	p. 584	Know ways to safeguard personal information
Consumer Privacy	Innovative Computing	p. 585	Be aware that your shopping behaviors may be recorded and tracked to create consumer profiles
	Link	eBook p. 585 or CourseMate	
Electronic Profiles	Text/Figure	p. 585	Be aware how direct marketers create electronic profiles
Spam	Text/Figure/FAQ	p. 587	Know how to reduce the amount of spam received
	FAQ Link	eBook p. 587 or CourseMate	
Phishing	Text/Figure/FAQ Ethics & Issues	pp. 587–588	Know how to protect yourself from phishing and pharming scams
	FAQ Link	eBook p. 588 or CourseMate	
Spyware and Adware	Text	p. 588	Know how to remove spyware and adware
Social Engineering	Text	p. 590	Be familiar with social engineering scams
Content Filtering	Text/Figure	pp. 590–591	Be familiar with issues of content filtering and Web filtering

Competent Digital Citizen

Goal: I would like to be knowledgeable and well-informed about computers, mobile devices, and related technology, so that I am digitally literate in my personal and professional use of digital devices.

Topic	Resource	Location	Now you should . . .
Security Risks	Text	p. 556	Know the definition of computer security risks
Cybercrime	Text	pp. 556–557	Be familiar with the categories of cybercriminals and punishments
	Ethics & Issues	p. 562	
Malware	Text/Figure/FAQ	pp. 558–559	Know the types of malware, how infections spread, and common symptoms of their infection
	FAQ Link	eBook p. 559 or CourseMate	
Botnets, DoS Attacks, Back Doors, Spoofing	Text and FAQ	pp. 562–563	Know the intent of botnets, DoS attacks, back doors, and spoofing
	Web Link	eBook p. 562 or CourseMate	
CAPTCHAs and RECAPTCHAs	Text/Figure Innovative Computing	p. 567	Know the purpose of CAPTCHAs and how RECAPTCHAs help digitize books and newspapers
	Link and Video	eBook p. 567 or CourseMate	
Brain Fingerprinting	Looking Ahead	p. 569	Know how brain fingerprints and behavior detection systems could be used in crime scene investigations
	Link and Video	eBook p. 569 or CourseMate	

Continued on next page

Continued from previous page

Topic	Resource	Location	Now you should . . .
Software Theft	Text	pp. 571 and 582	Be familiar with types of software theft
Encryption	Text/Figures	pp. 573–574	Know how encryption works
	Drag and Drop Figure 11-17	eBook p. 573 or CourseMate	
	Figure 11-18 Animation		
	Link and Video	eBook p. 592 or CourseMate	
Electrical Disturbances	Text	p. 575	Know the differences among noise, undervoltages, and overvoltages
War Driving	Text/Figure	p. 578	Be able to describe war driving
IP Rights	Text	p. 582	Be aware of intellectual property rights
Richard Stallman	Text	p. 593	Be familiar with Richard Stallman's copyleft concept
	Link and Video	eBook p. 593 or CourseMate	
Gene Spafford	Text	p. 593	Be familiar with Gene Spafford's role in computer security
	Link	eBook p. 593 or CourseMate	

Future Entrepreneur or Professional in a Digital Society

Goal: As I ponder my future, I envision myself as an entrepreneur or skilled professional using technology to support my business endeavors or job responsibilities. Along the way, I may interact with a variety of computer professionals — or I may just become one myself!

Topic	Resource	Location	Now you should . . .
Firewalls	Text	pp. 563–564	Be familiar with how enterprises use hardware firewalls
	Video	eBook p. 564 or CourseMate	
Intrusion Detection	Text	p. 564	Know why organizations use intrusion detection software
Honeypots	Text	p. 564	Know why an organization might use a honeypot
Authenticating Users	Text/Figures	pp. 565–568	Know how organizations identify and authenticate users through user names, passwords, possessed objects, and biometrics
	Web Link	eBook p. 568 or CourseMate	
Digital Forensics	Text	p. 569 and pp. 606–616	Know the purpose, uses, and steps in digital forensics
RTLS	Text	p. 570	Know the purpose and uses of real time location systems
	Web Link	eBook p. 570 or CourseMate	
BSA	Text	p. 572	Know the purpose of the Business Software Alliance
	Web Link	eBook p. 572 or CourseMate	
Digital Signatures and Certificates	Text/Figures	pp. 574–575	Know why organizations use digital signatures, digital certificates, and security protocols
UPS	Text/Figure	pp. 576–577	Know how organizations use UPS devices
Backing Up	Text	p. 577	Know the types of backups used by organizations
Employee Monitoring	Text Ethics & Issues	p. 590	Know issues surrounding employers monitoring employee communications

Continued on next page

Continued from previous page

Topic	Resource	Location	Now you should . . .
National and Local Security	Computer Usage @ Work	p. 591	Know how governments and businesses have implemented new security measures
	Link and Video	eBook p. 591 or CourseMate	
Digital Forensics Examiner	Exploring Computer Careers	CourseMate	Be familiar with responsibilities and education required for digital forensics examiners

Preparing for a Test

Visit the Computer Concepts CourseMate at **www.cengagebrain.com** and then navigate to the Chapter 11 Web Apps resource for this book to prepare for your test.

Does your class use the Computer Concepts CourseMate Web site? If so, prepare for your test by using the Flash Cards, Study Guide, and Practice Test Web apps — available for your smart phone or tablet.

If your class does not use the Computer Concepts CourseMate Web site or you prefer to use your book, you can prepare for the test by doing the Quiz Yourself activities on pages 569, 579, and 591; reading the Chapter Review on pages 594–595; ensuring you know the definitions for the terms on page 596; and completing the Checkpoint exercises on pages 597–598. You also should know the material identified in the Chapter 11 Study Guide that follows.

Chapter 11 Study Guide

This study guide identifies material you should know for the Chapter 11 exam. You may want to write the answers in a notebook, enter them on your digital device, record them into a phone, or highlight them in your book. Choose whichever method helps you remember the best.

1. Define the term, computer security risk.
2. Define the terms, computer crime and cybercrime.
3. Differentiate among a hacker, cracker, script kiddie, corporate spy, unethical employee, cyberextortionist, and cyberterrorist.
4. Describe the purpose of an online security service.
5. Differentiate among a computer virus, worm, Trojan horse, and rootkit.
6. Malware is short for _____.
7. Define payload. Identify various ways a payload is delivered.
8. Identify ways to safeguard against computer viruses and other malware.
9. Describe the purpose of an antivirus program. Explain techniques used by antivirus programs.
10. Define a botnet and a zombie. Describe ways to tell if a computer is a zombie or in a botnet.
11. DoS stands for _____. Explain how a DoS attack works. Identify reasons perpetrators claim to carry out a DoS attack.
12. Explain how a back door works.
13. Describe spoofing.
14. Define the term, firewall. Identify uses of firewalls.
15. Describe the purpose of intrusion detection software and honeypots.
16. AUP stands for _____.

17. Describe an access control.
18. Define the terms, user name and password. Identify ways to protect a password. Explain the purpose of a passphrase.
19. Explain the purpose and use of CAPTCHAs. Explain the benefits of RECAPTCHAs.
20. Give examples of possessed objects that might use a PIN.
21. Identify advantages and disadvantages of biometric devices.
22. Define digital forensics. Describe requirements of a digital forensics examiner.
23. Identify safeguards against hardware theft and vandalism.
24. Define software piracy. Explain the ways software manufacturers protect against software piracy.
25. Define a license agreement. Identify actions that are allowed and not allowed according to a license agreement.
26. Discuss the encryption process. Differentiate between private key and public key encryption.
27. Describe the purpose of digital signatures, digital certificates, transport layer security, secure HTTP, and VPN.
28. Identify causes of system failure.
29. Explain these electrical disturbances: noise, undervoltage, and overvoltage. Discuss surge protectors and UPSs.
30. Explain the options available for backing up computer resources.

Continued on next page

Continued from previous page

31. Describe the purpose of war driving. Identify ways to secure a wireless network.

32. RSI stands for _____. Identify two types of RSIs and precautions to prevent these injuries.

33. Describe symptoms of computer vision syndrome. Identify techniques to ease eyestrain.

34. Define ergonomics. Give examples of an ergonomically designed work area.

35. Identify symptoms of computer addiction.

36. Explain why users cannot assume information always is correct.

37. Describe intellectual property rights. Explain issues related to copyright law.

38. Define the purpose of an IT code of conduct.

39. Describe green computing strategies.

40. Identify ways to safeguard personal information.

41. Explain how electronic profiles are created.

42. Define cookie. Identify uses of cookies.

43. Describe spam, spyware, and adware. Explain ways to reduce spam, and remove spyware and adware.

44. Define phishing. Identify ways to protect yourself from phishing scams.

45. Identify common points in laws surrounding privacy.

46. Define social engineering.

47. Discuss issues of employee monitoring and content filtering.

48. Name two companies that sell products that protect computers and devices from malware, spam, and unauthorized access.

49. In digital forensics, identify the types of data and information that are examined and the software tasks that are performed.

Check This Out

As technology changes, you must keep up with updates, new products, breakthroughs, and recent advances to remain digitally literate. The list below identifies topics related to this chapter that you should explore to keep current. In parentheses beside each topic, you will find a search term to help begin your research using a search engine, such as Google.

For current news and information
Check us out on Facebook and Twitter. See your instructor or the Computer Concepts CourseMate for specific information.

1. **recent attempts to stop cybercrime activities** (search for: fighting cybercrime)

2. **latest CERT/CC security breach notices** (search for: CERT announcements)

3. **popular malware block and removal tools** (search for: top malware removal software)

4. **news of denial of service attacks** (search for: recent DoS DDoS attacks)

5. **popular antivirus programs** (search for: top antivirus programs)

6. **new biometric identification devices** (search for: biometric device systems)

7. **recent real time location system applications** (search for: latest RTLS)

8. **new products to curb hardware theft and vandalism** (search for: computer hardware theft deterrent)

9. **current Business Software Alliance efforts to fight software piracy** (search for: BSA piracy news)

10. **current encryption software** (search for: new encryption technology)

11. **new surge protectors and uninterruptible power supplies** (search for: popular surge protectors UPS)

12. **latest home wireless security network trends** (search for: home wireless network security software)

13. **current green computing initiatives** (search for: green computing concepts)

14. **recent phishing and smishing scams** (search for: phishing smishing attacks)

15. **updates about digital forensics procedures** (search for: digital forensics news)

Information System Development

Why Should I Learn About Information System Development?

"My school is starting to implement a new computer system, and the conversion process is taking a long time. Although the system sometimes does not work correctly for a few hours, some of the new features make registering for classes and checking my grades easy to do. Why should I learn about how this new computer system is being developed?"

True, you may be familiar with some of the material in this chapter, but do you know . . .

> "Why should I learn about how this new computer system is being developed?"

- Who is involved in developing a new information system? (p. 622, Who Participates in System Development?)
- Why people may lie when writing e-mail messages? (p. 627, Ethics & Issues)
- Which types of organizations are likely to use outside service providers? (p. 636, FAQ)
- How you can view billions of remote galaxy images on your computer? (p. 640, Looking Ahead)
- How computers are used to design and manufacture products in the textile industry? (p. 647, Computer Usage @ Work)
- Which nonprofit organization supports Wikipedia? (p. 649, Companies on the Cutting Edge)
- How to gather information in a personal interview? (p. 658 and Computer Concepts CourseMate, Learn How To)
- How to capture and print screen images? (Windows Exercises, Computer Concepts CourseMate)

For these answers and to discover much more information essential to this course, read Chapter 12 and visit the associated Computer Concepts CourseMate at www.cengagebrain.com.

Q & A How can I meet one or more of these goals?

Make use of the goal's resources for each chapter in the book and you should meet that goal by the end of the course.

Customize Your Learning Experience

Adapt this book to meet your needs by determining your goal. Would you like to be an informed digital consumer? A productive technology user? A safe user, protected from the risks in a digital world? A competent digital citizen? A future entrepreneur or professional in a digital society?

Every chapter in this Student Success Guide identifies resources targeted toward each of these goals, along with criteria to verify you understand the resources' content. Resources may be located in the textbook, on the Computer Concepts CourseMate Web site, in the interactive eBook, and on the Web.

Informed Digital Consumer

Goal: I would like to understand the terminology used in Web or print advertisements that sell computers, mobile devices, and related technology, as well as the jargon used by sales associates in computer or electronics stores, so that I can make informed purchasing decisions.

Topic	Resource	Location	Now you should . . .
Project Management Software	Text	p. 623	Know the purpose of project management software

Productive Technology User

Goal: I would like to learn ways that technology can benefit me at home, work, and school. I also would like to learn helpful techniques for using technology so that I can perform tasks more efficiently and be more productive in daily activities.

Topic	Resource	Location	Now you should . . .
Interviews	FAQ Link	eBook p. 626 or CourseMate	Know how to conduct various types of interviews and questions to expect as an interviewee
	Learn How To	pp. 658–659	

Continued on next page

Continued from previous page

Topic	Resource	Location	Now you should . . .
Project Request	Text	pp. 626–627	Know how to initiate a system development project
E-Zine	Text	p. 638	Be familiar with an e-zine and name popular ones
	Web Link	eBook p. 638 or CourseMate	
Prototype	Text	pp. 641–642	Know the purpose of a prototype
Wikimedia	Text	p. 649	Be familiar with Wikimedia Foundation's role with Wikipedia
	Link and Video	eBook p. 649 or CourseMate	
Windows Error Reporting	Windows Exercises	CourseMate	Know how to use Windows Error Reporting
Paint	Windows Exercises	CourseMate	Know how to use Paint to create a drawing
Capture Screen Images	Windows Exercises	CourseMate	Know how to capture screen images
Picnik	Web Apps	CourseMate	Know how to use Picnik to upload, crop, and e-mail photos

Safe User, Protected from the Risks in a Digital World

Goal: I would like to take measures to (1) protect my computers, devices, and data from loss, damage, or misuse; (2) minimize or prevent risks associated with using technology; and (3) minimize the environmental impact of using computers and related devices.

Topic	Resource	Location	Now you should . . .
Outsourcing	Ethics & Issues	p. 637	Be familiar with security issues related to outsourcing
Financial Web Site Vulnerabilities	FAQ	p. 646	Be aware of vulnerabilities associated with financial Web sites
Computer Security Plan	Text	p. 646	Be familiar with the elements of a computer security plan

Competent Digital Citizen

Goal: I would like to be knowledgeable and well-informed about computers, mobile devices, and related technology, so that I am digitally literate in my personal and professional use of digital devices.

Topic	Resource	Location	Now you should . . .
SDLC	Text/Figure	pp. 620–621	Be able to identify the phases in an SDLC
Documentation	Text	p. 625	Know the types of documentation generated in system development
Data and Information Gathering	Text/Figure and FAQ	pp. 625–626	Know the purpose of reviewing documentation, observing, surveying, interviewing, conducting JAD sessions, and researching; be able to explain the Hawthorne Effect
	Ethics & Issues		
	Video	eBook p. 625 or CourseMate	
Process Modeling	Text/Figures	pp. 631–634	Know the purpose and elements of tools used in process modeling: entity-relationship diagrams, data flow diagrams, and the project dictionary
	Web Link	eBook p. 631 or CourseMate	
	Drag and Drop Figures 12-7, 12-8, 12-10	eBook pp. 632–633 or CourseMate	
	Video	eBook p. 633 or CourseMate	

Continued on next page

Continued from previous page

Topic	Resource	Location	Now you should . . .
Object Modeling	Text/Figures	pp. 634–635	Be able to define an object, its properties, and methods; know the purpose of the UML; and be familiar with use case and class diagrams
	Web Link	eBook p. 634 or CourseMate	
Packaged vs. Custom Software	Text	pp. 635–636	Know the difference between packaged and custom software, and the difference between horizontal and vertical market software
	Web Link	eBook p. 636 or CourseMate	
LSST	Looking Ahead	p. 640	Know how the Large Synoptic Survey Telescope will provide a graphical view of the universe's evolution
	Link and Video	eBook p. 640 or CourseMate	
CASE Tools	Text/Figure	p. 642	Know the purpose and use of CASE tools
Phoenix Lander	Innovative Computing	p. 643	Be familiar with the role software played in the *Phoenix Mars Lander* Mission
	Link and Video	eBook p. 643 or CourseMate	
Conversion Strategies	Text/Figure	pp. 644–645	Know the differences between direct, parallel, phased, and pilot conversions
	Figure 12-22 Animation	eBook p. 645 or CourseMate	
Web App Vulnerabilities	FAQ Link	eBook p. 646, or Web Site Vulnerabilities link, CourseMate	Know how to test a Web application's vulnerabilities
Computers in the Textile Industry	Computer Usage @ Work	p. 647	Know how computers assist with the design and manufacturing of fabrics and clothing
	Link and Video	eBook p. 647 or CourseMate	
Benchmarking	Text/Figure	p. 648	Know how benchmarks are used to measure the performance of hardware or software
	Link and Video	eBook p. 648 or CourseMate	
	Drag and Drop Figure 12-23		
Ed Yourdon	Text	p. 649	Be familiar with Ed Yourdon's contributions to computer technology
	Link	eBook p. 649 or CourseMate	
Tom DeMarco	Text	p. 649	Be familiar with Tom Demarco's role with software development
	Link	eBook p. 649 or CourseMate	

Future Entrepreneur or Professional in a Digital Society

Goal: As I ponder my future, I envision myself as an entrepreneur or skilled professional using technology to support my business endeavors or job responsibilities. Along the way, I may interact with a variety of computer professionals — or I may just become one myself!

Topic	Resource	Location	Now you should . . .
System Development	Text/Figure	p. 620	Be able to describe an information system and system development
System Development Guidelines	Text	pp. 621–622	Know how system development groups activities into phases, involves users, and defines standards
System Development Participants	Text/Figure	pp. 622–623	Know the role of analysts, users, the steering committee, and others during system development
	Drag and Drop Figure 12-2	eBook p. 622 or CourseMate	

Continued on next page

Continued from previous page

Topic	Resource	Location	Now you should . . .
Project Management	Text/Figures and FAQ	pp. 623–624	Know how organizations use project management and the difference between Gantt and PERT charts
	Link and Video	eBook p. 623 or CourseMate	
	Web Links	eBook p. 624–625 or CourseMate	
	FAQ Link	eBook p. 624, or Project Failures link, CourseMate	
	Labs	CourseMate	
Feasibility	Text and FAQ	pp. 624–625 and p. 643	Know the tests organizations use to assess project feasibility
Planning Phase	Text	pp. 628–629	Know the major activities performed in the planning phase
Analysis Phase	Text	p. 629	Know the major activities performed in the analysis phase
Preliminary Investigation	Text/Figure	pp. 629–631	Know the purpose of the preliminary investigation and contents of the feasibility report
	Web Link	eBook p. 629 or CourseMate	
Detailed Analysis	Text	p. 631	Know the major activities performed during detailed analysis
Systems Analyst	FAQ	p. 631	Know the role of, responsibilities of, and education required for a systems analyst
	FAQ Link	eBook p. 631, or Systems Analyst link, CourseMate	
	Exploring Computer Careers	CourseMate	
System Proposal	Text	p. 635	Know the purpose of the system proposal
Outsourcing	Text/Figure	pp. 636–637	Know reasons organizations outsource software development
	FAQ Video	eBook p. 636 or CourseMate	
Design Phase	Text/Figures	pp. 638–640	Know the major activities performed in the design phase
RFQ, RFP, RFI	Text	p. 638	Know the difference of an RFQ, an RFP, and an RFI
VAR	Text and FAQ	pp. 638–639	Know the purpose of a value-added reseller
IT Consultants	Text and FAQ	p. 639	Know the role of IT consultants
	FAQ Link	eBook p. 639 or CourseMate	
Detailed Design	Text	pp. 640–641	Know the major activities performed during detailed design
Quality Review	Text	p. 642	Be familiar with quality review techniques
Implementation Phase	Text/Figures	pp. 643–645	Know the major activities performed during the implementation phase
Operation, Support, and Security Phase	Text	pp. 645–646	Know the major activities performed during the operation, support, and security phase
Chief Security Officer	Text	p. 646	Know the role and responsibilities of a chief security officer
	Web Link	eBook p. 646 or CourseMate	
Web Design	Labs	CourseMate	Be familiar with Web design principles
CSC	Text	p. 649	Be familiar with services provided by Computer Sciences Corporation
	Link	eBook p. 649 or CourseMate	

Preparing for a Test

Visit the Computer Concepts CourseMate at www.cengagebrain.com and then navigate to the Chapter 12 Web Apps resource for this book to prepare for your test.

Does your class use the Computer Concepts CourseMate Web site? If so, prepare for your test by using the Flash Cards, Study Guide, and Practice Test Web apps — available for your smart phone or tablet.

If your class does not use the Computer Concepts CourseMate Web site or you prefer to use your book, you can prepare for the test by doing the Quiz Yourself activities on pages 629, 637, and 647; reading the Chapter Review on pages 650–651; ensuring you know the definitions for the terms on page 652; and completing the Checkpoint exercises on pages 653–654. You also should know the material identified in the Chapter 12 Study Guide that follows.

Chapter 12 Study Guide

This study guide identifies material you should know for the Chapter 12 exam. You may want to write the answers in a notebook, enter them on your digital device, record them into a phone, or highlight them in your book. Choose whichever method helps you remember the best.

1. Describe an information system. Define system development.

2. SDLC stands for _____. Name the five phases that often are part of an SDLC.

3. Describe the three guidelines that system development should follow.

4. Describe the role of a systems analyst.

5. Define the purpose of a steering committee. Identify the composition of a project team.

6. Explain project management. Differentiate between a Gantt chart and a PERT chart. Explain how scope creep occurs.

7. Describe the purpose of change management.

8. Give examples of deliverables.

9. Define feasibility. Differentiate among operational feasibility, schedule feasibility, technical feasibility, and economic feasibility.

10. Describe data and information gathering techniques: review documentation, observe, survey, interview, conduct JAD sessions, and research.

11. Explain the Hawthorne Effect.

12. Differentiate between open-ended and closed-ended questions.

13. Explain the purpose of a project request. Name a synonym for project request.

14. Name and briefly describe the four major activities performed in the planning phase.

15. Name and briefly describe the two major activities performed in the analysis phase.

16. State the purpose of a feasibility study.

17. Name and briefly describe the three major activities performed in the detailed analysis phase.

18. Detailed analysis sometimes is called _____ design.

19. Describe user buy-in.

20. Process modeling sometimes is called _____.

21. Define process modeling. Describe the tools used during process modeling: entity-relationship diagrams, data flow diagrams, and the project dictionary.

22. Object modeling sometimes is called _____.

23. Define object modeling and objects. Give an example of an object. Define UML. Describe use case diagrams and class diagrams.

24. Identify the purpose of the system proposal.

25. Differentiate between packaged software and custom software. Describe outsourcing.

26. Differentiate between horizontal and vertical market software.

27. Name and briefly describe the two major activities performed in the design phase.

28. Name and briefly describe the four major tasks performed when acquiring hardware and software.

29. RFQ stands for _____. RFP stands for _____. RFI stands for _____. Differentiate among these three documents.

30. Describe the function of a VAR (value-added reseller).

31. Describe an IT consultant.

32. Detailed design sometimes is called _____.

33. Name and briefly describe the activities performed during detailed design.

34. Define the term, mockup.

35. Describe the purpose of a prototype.

36. Explain the purpose of CASE tools.

37. Describe the purpose of an inspection.

38. Name and briefly describe the four major activities performed in the implementation phase.

Continued on next page

Continued from previous page

39. Differentiate among a unit test, systems test, integration test, and acceptance test.

40. Describe various training methods.

41. Differentiate among direct conversion, parallel conversion, phased conversion, and pilot conversion.

42. Name and briefly describe the three major activities performed in the operation, support, and security phase.

43. Differentiate among corrective maintenance, adaptive maintenance, and perfective maintenance.

44. Identify the role of a CSO (chief security officer).

45. Identify the purpose of a computer security plan.

46. Define benchmark. Explain how benchmarks are used in the computer field.

47. Describe the purpose of the Wikimedia Foundation.

48. Identify Ed Yourdon's contributions to computer technology.

Check This Out

As technology changes, you must keep up with updates, new products, breakthroughs, and recent advances to remain digitally literate. The list below identifies topics related to this chapter that you should explore to keep current. In parentheses beside each topic, you will find a search term to help begin your research using a search engine, such as Google.

For current news and information
Check us out on Facebook and Twitter. See your instructor or the Computer Concepts CourseMate for specific information.

1. **latest information system developments** (search for: information system news)

2. **popular project management software** (search for: top project management software)

3. **recent Hawthorne Effect research** (search for: latest Hawthorne Effect studies)

4. **updates on developing effective JAD session questions** (search for: JAD questions)

5. **news on SDLC trends** (search for: SDLC planning)

6. **recent data flow diagram examples** (search for: data flow diagram news)

7. **popular unified modeling language tools** (search for: latest unified modeling language uses)

8. **latest outsourcing statistics** (search for: outsourcing trends)

9. **popular e-zine articles and publications** (search for: top e-zines)

10. **popular value-added resellers** (search for: top value-added software hardware resellers)

11. **current required IT consultant skills** (search for: IT consulting jobs)

12. **widely used conversion strategies** (search for: conversion strategies)

13. **updates on post-implementation system reviews** (search for: post-implementation system review news)

14. **new CAD and CAM systems for the textile industry** (search for: textile CAD CAM)

15. **latest news and views posted on the Wikimedia Foundation blog** (search for: Wikimedia blog)

Student Success Guide

Programming Languages and Program Development

Why Should I Learn About Programming Languages and Program Development?

"When my boss needs to update his payroll program, he hires a programmer to make changes. I would like to help, but the only software customizations I have made are adding some gadgets and widgets to my social networking home page. Other than assisting my boss, what else do I need to learn about programs and programming languages?"

True, you may be familiar with some of the material in this chapter, but do you know . . .

- Why some students learn to write computer viruses in their classes? (p. 681, Ethics & Issues)
- How Web page authoring software is used to create Web pages? (p. 685, Web Page Authoring Software)
- Why the term, bug, is used to refer to a computer error? (p. 696, Step 5 – Test Solution)
- How automakers use computers to streamline manufacturing? (p. 697, Computer Usage @ Work)
- Which software company develops the FIFA, Madden NFL, and Need for Speed video games? (p. 699, Companies on the Cutting Edge)
- How to evaluate a graphical user interface? (p. 708 and Computer Concepts CourseMate, Learn How To)
- How to adjust the speed of your keyboard? (Windows Exercises, Computer Concepts CourseMate)
- How developers create Web 2.0 applications for social networks and the cloud? (p. 712, Web 2.0 Program Development Special Feature)

For these answers and to discover much more information essential to this course, read Chapter 13 and visit the associated Computer Concepts CourseMate at www.cengagebrain.com.

Q & A
How can I meet one or more of these goals?

Make use of the goal's resources for each chapter in the book and you should meet that goal by the end of the course.

Customize Your Learning Experience

Adapt this book to meet your needs by determining your goal. Would you like to be an informed digital consumer? A productive technology user? A safe user, protected from the risks in a digital world? A competent digital citizen? A future entrepreneur or professional in a digital society?

Every chapter in this Student Success Guide identifies resources targeted toward each of these goals, along with criteria to verify you understand the resources' content. Resources may be located in the textbook, on the Computer Concepts CourseMate Web site, in the interactive eBook, and on the Web.

Informed Digital Consumer

Goal: I would like to understand the terminology used in Web or print advertisements that sell computers, mobile devices, and related technology, as well as the jargon used by sales associates in computer or electronics stores, so that I can make informed purchasing decisions.

Topic	Resource	Location	Now you should . . .
Flowcharting Software	Text/Figure	p. 691–692	Be familiar with uses of flowcharting software
	Web Link	eBook p. 692 or CourseMate	
EA	Text	p. 699	Be familiar with entertainment products by Electronic Arts
	Link	eBook p. 699 or CourseMate	
	Video	At the Movies, CourseMate	

Productive Technology User

Goal: I would like to learn ways that technology can benefit me at home, work, and school. I also would like to learn helpful techniques for using technology so that I can perform tasks more efficiently and be more productive in daily activities.

Topic	Resource	Location	Now you should . . .
Online Calculators	Innovative Computing	p. 668	Know popular calculators on the Web
	Link	eBook p. 668 or CourseMate	
4GLs	Text/Figure and FAQ	pp. 674–675	Know the uses of 4GLs and SQL
	FAQ Link	eBook p. 675, or SQL link, CourseMate	
Application Generators	Text/Figure	p. 676	Be familiar with the use of application generators
Macros	Text/Figure	pp. 676–677	Know the purpose of macros and how to create them
	Web Link	eBook p. 677 or CourseMate	
Earth Album	Innovative Computing	p. 684	Know the purpose of the Earth Album mashup
Mashups	Videos	eBook p. 684 or CourseMate	Be able to state examples and uses of mashups
		eBook p. 715 or CourseMate	
Beta Testers	Web Link	eBook p. 696 or CourseMate	Know the role of beta testers
Creating Web Pages	Labs	CourseMate	Know how to create Web pages (formatting, graphics, backgrounds, links)
Program Files	Windows Exercises	CourseMate	Know how to search for executable files
Keyboard Speed	Windows Exercises	CourseMate	Know how to adjust keyboard speed
Loans	Windows Exercises	CourseMate	Know how to use the Loan Payment Calculator program
Google Earth	Web Apps	CourseMate	Know how to use Google Earth to view locations and satellite images

Safe User, Protected from the Risks in a Digital World

Goal: I would like to take measures to (1) protect my computers, devices, and data from loss, damage, or misuse; (2) minimize or prevent risks associated with using technology; and (3) minimize the environmental impact of using computers and related devices.

Topic	Resource	Location	Now you should . . .
Macro Security	Ethics & Issues	p. 677	Be aware of security threats surrounding macros
ActiveX Controls and Plug-Ins	FAQ	p. 680	Know when to install or disable a control or plug-in
	Video	eBook p. 680 or CourseMate	
Ethical Hacking	Ethics & Issues	p. 681	Be aware that some colleges teach hacking and know the meaning of ethical hacking
	Video	eBook p. 681 or CourseMate	
Digital Facelifts	Ethics & Issues	p. 688	Know the issues surrounding digital facelifts

Competent Digital Citizen

Goal: I would like to be knowledgeable and well-informed about computers, mobile devices, and related technology, so that I am digitally literate in my personal and professional use of digital devices.

Topic	Resource	Location	Now you should . . .
Programming Lang.	Text/Figure	p. 664	Be able to describe programming languages
Low- vs. High-Level	Text	pp. 664–665	Know the difference between low-level and high-level languages
Machine Language	Text/Figure	p. 665	Know the purpose of machine language
Assembly Language	Text/Figure	pp. 665–666	Know the purpose of an assembly language
Source Program	Text	p. 666	Be able to define source program
Procedural Languages	Text	p. 666	Describe procedural languages
Compilers vs. Interpreters	Text/Figures	pp. 666–667	Be able to differentiate between compilers and interpreters
	Drag and Drop Figures 13-4 and 13-5	eBook p. 667 or CourseMate	
C and COBOL	Text/Figures	pp. 668–669	Know the uses of C and COBOL
	Web Link	eBook p. 668 or CourseMate	
OOP Languages/Tools	Text/Figures	pp. 669–674	Describe object-oriented programming languages, RAD, and IDE
Java, .NET, C++, C#, and F#	Text/Figure	pp. 670–671	Know the characteristics and uses of Java, .NET, C++, C#, and F#
	Web Link	eBook p. 670 or CourseMate	
Visual Studio	Text/Figure	pp. 671–673	Know the purpose of and languages in the Visual Studio suite, visual programming, and user interface design
	Web Link	eBook p. 671 or CourseMate	
	Labs	CourseMate	
	Learn How To	pp. 708–709	
Delphi and PowerBuilder	Text/Figures	pp. 673–675	Know the uses of Delphi and PowerBuilder
Classic Programming Languages	Text/Figure	p. 675	Know the purpose of several classic programming languages
HTML, XHTML, XML, and WML	Text/Figures	pp. 678–679	Know the characteristics and uses of HTML, XHTML, XML, and WML
	Link and Video	eBook p. 679 or CourseMate	
Scripts, Applets, Servlets, and ActiveX	Text	p. 680	Know the differences among scripts, applets, servlets, and ActiveX controls
	FAQ Link	eBook p. 680, or Web Browser Prompts link, CourseMate	
CGI Scripts	Text/Figure	pp. 680–681	Know the purpose of CGI scripts
	Drag and Drop Figure 13-19	eBook p. 681 or CourseMate	
Scripting Languages	Text/Figure	pp. 682–683	Know the purpose of JavaScript, Perl, PHP, Rexx, Tcl, and VBScript
	Web Link	eBook p. 682 or CourseMate	
Sandbox	FAQ	p. 683	Know why developers use sandboxes
	FAQ Link	eBook p. 683, or Sandboxes link, CourseMate	

Continued on next page

Continued from previous page

Topic	Resource	Location	Now you should . . .
Dynamic HTML	Text	p. 683	Know the characteristics and uses of DHTML
	Web Link	eBook p. 683 or CourseMate	
Ruby on Rails	Text	p. 683	Be familiar with the purpose of Ruby on Rails
Web 2.0 Development	Text	p. 684	Be familiar with tools and languages used to develop Web 2.0 sites and the purpose of APIs
	Web Link	eBook p. 684 or CourseMate	
Web Page Authoring	Text	p. 685	Know about Dreamweaver, Expression Web, Flash, and SharePoint Designer
Multimedia Develop.	Text/Figure	p. 685	Be familiar with the purpose of ToolBook and Director
Program Development	Text/Figures	pp. 686–697	Know and be able to describe the steps in the program development life cycle and how it relates to the SDLC
	Drag and Drop Figure 13-23	eBook p. 686 or CourseMate	
Structured Design	Text/Figure	p. 688	Know the purpose of and charts used in structured design
Object-Oriented Design	Text/Figure	p. 689	Know the purpose of and charts used in object-oriented design
	Web Link	eBook p. 689 or CourseMate	
Control Structures	Text/Figures	pp. 689–690	Know the differences among sequence, selection, and repetition control structures
	Figure 13-31 Animation	eBook p. 690 or CourseMate	
Design Tools	Text/Figures	pp. 691–693	Know the purpose of program flowcharts, pseudocode, and the UML diagrams
	Figure Video	eBook p. 691 or CourseMate	
	Drag and Drop Figures 13-32 and 13-36	eBook p. 691 and 693 or CourseMate	
Test Data	Text and FAQ	pp. 693–694	Be familiar with types of test data and desk checking steps
	FAQ Link	eBook p. 694, or Test Data link, CourseMate	
Program Errors	Text	pp. 695–696	Know the difference between syntax and logic errors
Documentation	FAQ	p. 697	Know the types of documentation to include with programs
	FAQ Link	eBook p. 697 or CourseMate	
Acid3 Browser Test	Text/Figure	p. 698	Be familiar with the purpose of the Acid3 Browser Test
	Link and Video	eBook p. 698 or CourseMate	
Sun	Text	p. 699	Be familiar with Sun's products and services
	Link	eBook p. 699 or CourseMate	
Alan Kay	Text	p. 693	Be familiar with Alan Kay's computing research
	Link and Video	eBook p. 699 or CourseMate	
James Gosling	Text	p. 699	Be familiar with James Gosling's contributions to the computer field
	Link and Video	eBook p. 699 or CourseMate	
Web 2.0 Development	Text/Figures	pp. 712–717	Be familiar with tools used in Web 2.0 program development

Future Entrepreneur or Professional in a Digital Society

Goal: As I ponder my future, I envision myself as an entrepreneur or skilled professional using technology to support my business endeavors or job responsibilities. Along the way, I may interact with a variety of computer professionals — or I may just become one myself!

Topic	Resource	Location	Now you should . . .
Programmer	Text	p. 664	Know the role and responsibilities of and the education required for a computer programmer
	Exploring Computer Careers	CourseMate	
Programming Language Trends	Looking Ahead	p. 675	Be familiar with trends related to programming languages
	Link and Video	eBook p. 675 or CourseMate	
Popular Web Programming Languages	FAQ	p. 683	Be familiar with popular Web programming languages
	FAQ Link	eBook p. 683 or Web Programming Languages link, CourseMate	
Programming Team	Text	p. 687	Know the purpose of a programming team
Computers in Manufacturing	Computer Usage @ Work	p. 697	Know how computers are used in the manufacture of cars
	Link and Video	eBook p. 697 or CourseMate	

Preparing for a Test

Visit the Computer Concepts CourseMate at **www.cengagebrain.com** and then navigate to the Chapter 13 Web Apps resource for this book to prepare for your test.

Does your class use the Computer Concepts CourseMate Web site? If so, prepare for your test by using the Flash Cards, Study Guide, and Practice Test Web apps — available for your smart phone or tablet.

If your class does not use the Computer Concepts CourseMate Web site or you prefer to use your book, you can prepare for the test by doing the Quiz Yourself activities on pages 674, 686, and 697; reading the Chapter Review on pages 700–701; ensuring you know the definitions for the terms on page 702; and completing the Checkpoint exercises on pages 703–704. You also should know the material identified in the Chapter 13 Study Guide that follows.

Chapter 13 Study Guide

This study guide identifies material you should know for the Chapter 13 exam. You may want to write the answers in a notebook, enter them on your digital device, record them into a phone, or highlight them in your book. Choose whichever method helps you remember the best.

1. Define computer program and programming language.

2. Another term for programmer is _____.

3. Differentiate between low-level and high-level languages.

4. Define machine language.

5. Describe how a programmer writes assembly language instructions and the purpose of an assembler.

6. Define source program.

7. Describe how a programmer writes procedural language instructions.

8. Differentiate between a compiler and an interpreter.

9. Define the term, algorithm.

10. Identify uses of C and COBOL.

11. Define an object. Describe advantages of object-oriented programming languages.

12. RAD stands for _____. Describe RAD.

13. IDE stands for _____. Identify tools in an IDE.

14. Name the company that developed Java.

15. Describe the purpose of the .NET Framework.

16. Briefly discuss characteristics of C++, C#, and F#.

17. Describe Visual Studio. Differentiate among Visual Basic, Visual C++, and Visual C#.

18. Define visual programming language.

Continued on next page

Continued from previous page

19. Briefly describe the use of Delphi and PowerBuilder.

20. 4GL stands for _____.

21. Describe how a programmer writes nonprocedural language instructions.

22. Describe the purpose of SQL.

23. Describe the purpose of application generators.

24. Define macro. Describe two techniques for creating macros.

25. Describe the purpose of HTML and XHTML. Define a tag.

26. Describe the purpose of XML and WML. Explain the purpose of style sheets.

27. Identify the use of RSS 2.0 and ATOM.

28. Discuss and identify uses of scripts, applets, servlets, and ActiveX controls.

29. Identify the purpose of counters and image maps.

30. Describe the purpose of a CGI script.

31. Differentiate among JavaScript, Perl, PHP, Rexx, Tcl, and VBScript.

32. Describe the purpose of a sandbox.

33. Identify the purpose of DHTML. Describe how it uses the document object model, cascading style sheets, and scripting languages.

34. Identify the use of Ruby on Rails. Describe the purpose of Ajax.

35. API stands for _____. Define mashup. Explain the relationship between API and mashup.

36. Describe the purpose of Web page authoring software. Name some examples.

37. Describe the purpose of multimedia authoring software. Name some examples.

38. PDLC stands for _____. Name the six steps in the PDLC. Identify tasks performed during each step.

39. Define solution algorithm.

40. Differentiate between structured design and object-oriented design.

41. Differentiate between sequence, selection, and repetition control structures.

42. Describe the purpose of flowcharts, pseudocode, and the UML.

43. Identify steps performed by programmers during a desk check.

44. Describe extreme programming.

45. Differentiate a syntax error from a logic error.

46. Define the terms, bug and debugging.

47. Identify the type of software developed by Electronic Arts.

48. Identify an advantage of Web 2.0 program development. Describe the tiers in Web applications. Differentiate Web 2.0 program development from traditional Web page development.

Check This Out

As technology changes, you must keep up with updates, new products, breakthroughs, and recent advances to remain digitally literate. The list below identifies topics related to this chapter that you should explore to keep current. In parentheses beside each topic, you will find a search term to help begin your research using a search engine, such as Google.

For current news and information
Check us out on Facebook and Twitter. See your instructor or the Computer Concepts CourseMate for specific information.

1. **widely used programming languages** (search for: popular programming languages)

2. **high-level programming languages to know** (search for: best high-level programming learn)

3. **current uses of assembly languages** (search for: assembly code example)

4. **new object-oriented programming languages** (search for: recent OOP languages)

5. **popular rapid application development components** (search for: top RAD environment tools)

6. **new Microsoft Visual Studio tools** (search for: Visual Studio features)

7. **recent visual programming languages** (search for: latest visual programming languages)

8. **new fourth-generation languages** (search for: latest fourth-generation programming languages)

9. **widely used Visual Basic for Applications macros** (search for: popular VBA macro examples)

10. **popular RSS and ATOM XML applications** (search for: XML applications RSS ATOM)

11. **new common gateway interface scripts** (search for: CGI script examples)

12. **popular Web programming languages** (search for: top Web programming languages)

13. **widely used Web page authoring software** (search for: popular Web page authoring programs)

14. **popular flowcharting programs** (search for: best flowcharting software)

15. **latest Web 2.0 program development technologies** (search for: Web 2.0 program development toolkits)

Enterprise Computing

Why Should I Learn About Enterprise Computing?

"My neighbor owns a small manufacturing business, and I often assist him on weekends by billing his customers and updating his budget. I back up the data on his computer to a USB flash drive and plan to expand his business interactions over the Internet. These computer functions seem adequate, so why should I learn about enterprise computing?"

True, you may be familiar with some of the material in this chapter, but do you know . . .

"Why should I learn about enterprise computing?"

- How various units function within a business? (p. 726, Information Systems in the Enterprise)
- Why practically everyone soon may be using cloud computing? (p. 746, Cloud and Grid Computing)
- What hardware you can use to back up data on your computer continuously? (p. 755, FAQ)
- How PS3s are used in astrophysics labs to study black holes? (p. 756, Innovative Computing)
- How municipalities use computers to enhance services? (p. 757, Computer Usage @ Work)
- Which YouTube cofounder created PayPal's original logo? (p. 759, Companies on the Cutting Edge)
- How to use Skype to make unlimited calls? (p. 768 and Computer Concepts CourseMate, Learn How To)
- How to create a desktop shortcut to print? (Windows Exercises, Computer Concepts CourseMate)

For these answers and to discover much more information essential to this course, read Chapter 14 and visit the associated Computer Concepts CourseMate at www.cengagebrain.com.

Customize Your Learning Experience

Q & A How can I meet one or more of these goals?

Make use of the goal's resources for each chapter in the book and you should meet that goal by the end of the course.

Adapt this book to meet your needs by determining your goal. Would you like to be an informed digital consumer? A productive technology user? A safe user, protected from the risks in a digital world? A competent digital citizen? A future entrepreneur or professional in a digital society?

Every chapter in this Student Success Guide identifies resources targeted toward each of these goals, along with criteria to verify you understand the resources' content. Resources may be located in the textbook, on the Computer Concepts CourseMate Web site, in the interactive eBook, and on the Web.

Informed Digital Consumer

Goal: I would like to understand the terminology used in Web or print advertisements that sell computers, mobile devices, and related technology, as well as the jargon used by sales associates in computer or electronics stores, so that I can make informed purchasing decisions.

Topic	Resource	Location	Now you should . . .
Order Processing	Text/Figures	pp. 772–781	Be familiar with the steps involved with order processing from the customer creating a shopping cart to the customer receiving the order and requesting support

Productive Technology User

Goal: I would like to learn ways that technology can benefit me at home, work, and school. I also would like to learn helpful techniques for using technology so that I can perform tasks more efficiently and be more productive in daily activities.

Topic	Resource	Location	Now you should . . .
Telecommuting	Ethics & Issues	p. 745	Know the benefits of telecommuting
	Video	eBook p. 745 or CourseMate	
E-Commerce	Text	p. 747	Know the online services that users find beneficial: e-retail, finance, travel, entertainment and media, and health
	Drag and Drop Figure 14-25	eBook p. 747 or CourseMate	
Computers in Municipal Services	Computer Usage @ Work	p. 757	Know how you interact with or benefit from computers in various municipal services
	Link and Video	eBook p. 757 or CourseMate	
VoIP	Learn How To	pp. 768–769 and CourseMate	Know how to use VoIP (Voice over Internet Protocol)
Changing Windows Views	Windows Exercises	CourseMate	Know how to change views in Windows
Desktop Shortcuts	Windows Exercises	CourseMate	Know how to create a desktop shortcut in Windows
Sounds Cards and Audio Devices	Windows Exercises	CourseMate	Know how to determine the brand and model of sound cards and audio devices on your computer
Microsoft Office Web Apps	Web Apps	CourseMate	Know how to use Microsoft Office Web Apps to create, edit, and share documents, workbooks, presentations, and notes

Safe User, Protected from the Risks in a Digital World

Goal: I would like to take measures to (1) protect my computers, devices, and data from loss, damage, or misuse; (2) minimize or prevent risks associated with using technology; and (3) minimize the environmental impact of using computers and related devices.

Topic	Resource	Location	Now you should . . .
Personal Information	FAQ	p. 730	Know to be careful when supplying personal information to companies
	FAQ Link	eBook p. 730, or Sharing Personal Information link, CourseMate	
Online Purchases	Ethics & Issues	p. 747	Be familiar with ways to safeguard online purchases
Energy Consumption	FAQ	p. 748	Be familiar with power-saving practices in data centers
	FAQ Link	eBook p. 748, or Energy Reduction link, CourseMate	
Backup Procedures	Text/Figure and FAQ	pp. 754–755	Know the difference in various backup methods: full, differential, incremental, selective, and continuous
	Drag and Drop Figure 14-33	eBook p. 754 or CourseMate	
Disaster Recovery Plan	Text	pp. 755–756	Know the components of a disaster recovery plan
	Link and Video	eBook p. 756 or CourseMate	

Competent Digital Citizen

Goal: I would like to be knowledgeable and well-informed about computers, mobile devices, and related technology, so that I am digitally literate in my personal and professional use of digital devices.

Topic	Resource	Location	Now you should . . .
Portals	Text/Figure	pp. 740–741	Know the purpose and use of a portal
Data Warehouses	Text/Figure	pp. 741–742	Know the purpose and use of data warehouses
EDI	Text	p. 742	Know the purpose of electronic data interchange
Extranets	Text	p. 742	Know the benefits of an extranet
Web Services	Text/Figure	pp. 742–743	Know how Web services work
	Drag and Drop Figure 14-22	eBook p. 743 or CourseMate	
	Web Link		
SOA	Text	p. 743	Know the purpose of a service-oriented architecture
Document Management Systems	Text	p. 743	Know the benefits of document management systems
Workflow	Text/Figure	p. 744	Be familiar with workflow and workflow applications
VPN	Text/Figure	pp. 744–745	Know the purpose of a virtual private network
Virtualization	Text and FAQ	pp. 745–746	Be familiar with benefits of and various types of virtualization
	Links and Video	eBook p. 746 or CourseMate	
Cloud Computing	Text	p. 746	Be familiar with trends in cloud computing
	Looking Ahead		
	Video	eBook p. 746 or CourseMate	
Grid Computing	Text	p. 746	Know the purpose of grid computing
RAID	Text/Figure	pp. 748–749	Know how RAID works
	Figure 14-26 Animation	eBook p. 748 or CourseMate	
NAS and SAN	Text/Figure	pp. 749–750	Know the purpose of network attached storage and storage area networks
	Web Link	eBook p. 750 or CourseMate	
Blade Servers	Text/Figure and FAQ	p. 751	Know the purpose and advantages of blade servers
Thin Clients	Text/Figure	p. 752	Know the purpose of a thin client
High-Availability Systems	Text/Figure	pp. 752–753	Be familiar with uses of high-availability systems and the purpose of redundant components
Scalability	Text	p. 753	Know the definition of scalability
Interoperability	Text	pp. 753–754	Know the definition of interoperability
PS3 Gravity Grid	Innovative Computing	p. 756	Know how PS3s are simulating black hole activity
	Link	eBook p. 756 or CourseMate	

Continued on next page

Continued from previous page

Topic	Resource	Location	Now you should . . .
Neural Networks	Text/Figure	p. 758	Know how neural networks work and uses of neural networks
	Link and Video	eBook p. 758 or CourseMate	
EMC	Text	p. 759	Be familiar with EMC's products and services
	Link	eBook p. 759 or CourseMate	
IBM	Text	p. 759	Be familiar with IBM's products and services
	Link	eBook p. 759 or CourseMate	
Chad Hurley	Text	p. 759	Be familiar with Chad Hurley's contributions to technology
	Link and Video	eBook p. 759 or CourseMate	
Anita Borg	Text	p. 759	Be familiar with Anita Borg's role with women in technology
	Link	eBook p. 759 or CourseMate	

Future Entrepreneur or Professional in a Digital Society

Goal: As I ponder my future, I envision myself as an entrepreneur or skilled professional using technology to support my business endeavors or job responsibilities. Along the way, I may interact with a variety of computer professionals — or I may just become one myself!

Topic	Resource	Location	Now you should . . .
Enterprise Computing	Text/Figure	pp. 720–722	Know the meaning of enterprise computing
Enterprise Types	Text	p. 722	Be familiar with various types of enterprises
Organizational Structure	Text/Figure	p. 723	Know the difference between supporting and core activities, and the difference between a decentralized and centralized IT approach
Levels of Users	Text/Figure	p. 724	Know the difference between decision levels and job titles for executive management, middle management, operational management, and nonmanagement employees
	Drag and Drop Figure 14-3	eBook p. 724 or CourseMate	
Management	Text	pp. 725–726	Know how managers plan, organize, lead, and control; know how they use business intelligence, business process management, and business process automation
	Drag and Drop Figure 14-4	eBook p. 725 or CourseMate	
	Web Link		
Functional Units	Text/Figures	pp. 726–732	Know the role of functional units in most organizations: accounting and finance, human resources, engineering, manufacturing, quality control, marketing, sales, distribution, customer service, and information technology
	Drag and Drop Figure 14-6	eBook p. 727 or CourseMate	
	Figure Video	eBook p. 730 or CourseMate	
	Web Link	eBook p. 731 or CourseMate	
General Information Systems	Text/Figures	pp. 732–737	Be able to describe each type of general information system: office information system (OIS), transaction processing system (TPS), management information system (MIS), decision support system (DSS), and expert system
Integrated Information Systems	Text/Figures	pp. 737–739	Be able to describe each type of integrated information system: customer relationship management (CRM), enterprise resource planning (ERP), and content management system (CMS)
	Web Link	eBook p. 738 or CourseMate	

Continued on next page

Continued from previous page

Topic	Resource	Location	Now you should . . .
Data Centers	Text	p. 740	Be aware of the purpose of a data center and be familiar with some examples
	Innovative Computing		
	Link and Video	eBook p. 740 or CourseMate	
	Web Link		
	Video	At the Movies, CourseMate	
Wikis	FAQ	p. 742	Know why enterprises use wikis
Enterprise Storage	Text/Figure	pp. 750–751	Be familiar with storage strategies used by enterprises
Sarbanes-Oxley Act	Ethics & Issues	p. 751	Be familiar with financial reporting requirements defined by the Sarbanes-Oxley Act
CIO	Exploring Computer Careers	CourseMate	Be familiar with the responsibilities of and education required for a chief information officer (CIO)

Preparing for a Test

Visit the Computer Concepts CourseMate at www.cengagebrain.com and then navigate to the Chapter 14 Web Apps resource for this book to prepare for your test.

Does your class use the Computer Concepts CourseMate Web site? If so, prepare for your test by using the Flash Cards, Study Guide, and Practice Test Web apps — available for your smart phone or tablet.

If your class does not use the Computer Concepts CourseMate Web site or you prefer to use your book, you can prepare for the test by doing the Quiz Yourself activities on pages 740, 748, and 757; reading the Chapter Review on pages 760–761; ensuring you know the definitions for the terms on page 762; and completing the Checkpoint exercises on pages 763–764. You also should know the material identified in the Chapter 14 Study Guide that follows.

Chapter 14 Study Guide

This study guide identifies material you should know for the Chapter 14 exam. You may want to write the answers in a notebook, enter them on your digital device, record them into a phone, or highlight them in your book. Choose whichever method helps you remember the best.

1. Define enterprise computing.

2. Know the purpose of these types of enterprises: retail, manufacturing, service, wholesale, government, educational, and transportation.

3. Differentiate between supporting and core business activities.

4. Differentiate between a decentralized and centralized approach to information technology.

5. Identify the types of decisions and sample job titles of executive management, middle management, operational management, and nonmanagement employees.

6. Describe how managers plan, organize, lead, and control.

7. Define business intelligence, business process management, and business process automation.

8. Describe the purpose of and software used by these business functional units: accounting and finance, human resources, engineering or product development, manufacturing, quality control, marketing, sales, distribution, customer service, and information technology.

9. ERM stands for _____.

10. MRP stands for _____. Describe MRP.

11. Describe these general information systems: office information system (OIS), transaction processing system (TPS), management information system (MIS), decision support system (DSS), and expert system.

12. Differentiate online transaction processing (OLTP) from online analytical processing (OLAP).

13. Define the purpose of an executive information system (EIS).

Continued on next page

Continued from previous page

14. AI stands for _____.

15. Describe AI.

16. Describe these integrated information systems: customer relationship management (CRM), enterprise resource planning (ERP), and content management systems (CMS).

17. Define data center.

18. Describe the purpose and capabilities of a portal.

19. Describe how data warehouses work.

20. Define click stream.

21. Explain reasons enterprises use wikis.

22. Identify uses of extranets.

23. Describe the purpose of Web services.

24. Identify a benefit of using a service-oriented architecture.

25. Identify benefits of document management systems.

26. Describe a workflow and a workflow application.

27. Describe the purpose of a virtual private network (VPN).

28. Define virtualization. Give examples.

29. Identify benefits of cloud computing.

30. Define grid computing.

31. Explain the purpose of these e-commerce market segments: e-retail, finance, travel, entertainment and media, and health.

32. Identify ways to shop safely online.

33. Define legacy system.

34. Identify techniques data centers use to reduce energy consumption.

35. Describe the purpose of RAID. Differentiate between mirroring and striping.

36. Describe the purpose of network attached storage and storage area networks.

37. Identify the goal of an enterprise storage system. Describe storage techniques used by enterprise storage systems.

38. State the purpose of the Sarbanes-Oxley Act.

39. Describe a blade server.

40. Describe a thin client.

41. Define high-availability system and redundant components.

42. Explain scalability and interoperability.

43. Differentiate among these backup methods: full, differential, incremental, selective, and continuous.

44. Describe the components of a disaster recovery plan.

45. Define neural network. Briefly describe how neural networks work.

46. Identify services provided by EMC.

47. _____ cofounded YouTube.

48. Briefly describe the steps in order processing.

Check This Out

As technology changes, you must keep up with updates, new products, breakthroughs, and recent advances to remain digitally literate. The list below identifies topics related to this chapter that you should explore to keep current. In parentheses beside each topic, you will find a search term to help begin your research using a search engine, such as Google.

1. **new enterprise organizational structure developments** (search for: enterprise organization structure)

2. **recent iPad and tablet computer uses in corporations** (search for: iPad tablet corporations)

3. **recent business process management developments** (search for: business process management news)

4. **updates on information systems research** (search for: information system news)

5. **new software and information systems used in human resources** (search for: HRIS software)

6. **recent models created using 3-D visualization** (search for: 3D visualization)

7. **popular quality control programs** (search for: latest quality control software)

8. **latest online transaction processing applications** (search for: online transaction processing news)

9. **top content management systems** (search for: best content management systems)

10. **widely used Web service business applications** (search for: top business Web services)

11. **latest predictions on the future of cloud computing** (search for: trends cloud computing)

12. **widely used enterprise hardware** (search for: enterprise hardware storage)

13. **updates on backup and recovery methods** (search for: backup recovery procedures news)

14. **new real-life neural network uses** (search for: neural networks applications)

15. **latest news about IBM enterprise technology** (search for: IBM enterprise systems)

For current news and information
Check us out on Facebook and Twitter. See your instructor or the Computer Concepts CourseMate for specific information.

Why Should I Learn About Computer Careers and Certification?

"I have enjoyed discovering many facets of the computer field in this course. I would like to continue learning about technology, especially because I have heard that jobs for computer majors are available in a variety of fields throughout the world. How can I learn more about employment in the computer industry and required certifications?"

You may be familiar with some of the material in this chapter, but do you know . . .

"How can I learn more about employment in the computer industry and required certifications?"

- How younger and older workers can blend their skills in the office? (p. 786, Looking Ahead)
- How lucrative starting salaries are for computer science majors? (p. 787, FAQ)
- When you can copy software legally? (p. 791, Ethics & Issues)
- How publishers use computers to develop and print textbooks? (p. 809, Computer Usage @ Work)
- Which Microsoft executive was Bill Gates's college classmate? (p. 811, Technology Trailblazers)
- How to create a video resume? (p. 820 and Computer Concepts CourseMate, Learn How To)
- How to plan regular hard disk maintenance? (Windows Exercises, Computer Concepts CourseMate)
- Which digital products affect most facets of life? (p. 824, Living Digitally Special Feature)

For these answers and to discover much more information essential to this course, read Chapter 15 and visit the associated Computer Concepts CourseMate at www.cengagebrain.com.

Q & A ◄ How can I meet one or more of these goals?

Make use of the goal's resources for each chapter in the book and you should meet that goal by the end of the course.

Customize Your Learning Experience

Adapt this book to meet your needs by determining your goal. Would you like to be an informed digital consumer? A productive technology user? A safe user, protected from the risks in a digital world? A competent digital citizen? A future entrepreneur or professional in a digital society?

Every chapter in this Student Success Guide identifies resources targeted toward each of these goals, along with criteria to verify you understand the resources' content. Resources may be located in the textbook, on the Computer Concepts CourseMate Web site, in the interactive eBook, and on the Web.

Informed Digital Consumer

Goal: I would like to understand the terminology used in Web or print advertisements that sell computers, mobile devices, and related technology, as well as the jargon used by sales associates in computer or electronics stores, so that I can make informed purchasing decisions.

Topic	Resource	Location	Now you should . . .
Online Classes	Innovative Computing Link and Video	eBook p. 794 or CourseMate	Know about one school's online offering
Living Digitally	Text/Figures	pp. 824–830	Be familiar with audio, video, recording, gaming, and digital home products you may find useful

Productive Technology User

Goal: I would like to learn ways that technology can benefit me at home, work, and school. I also would like to learn helpful techniques for using technology so that I can perform tasks more efficiently and be more productive in daily activities.

Topic	Resource	Location	Now you should . . .
Trade School	Text	p. 794	Know the benefits of attending a trade school
	Web Link	eBook p. 794 or CourseMate	
Colleges and Universities	Text/Figure	pp. 794–795	Know the differences among computer disciplines at colleges or universities
	Drag and Drop Figure 15-8	eBook p. 795 or CourseMate	
	Web Link		
Searching for a Job	Text/Figure	pp. 796–797	Know how to search for a job online
	Figure 15-10 Animation	eBook p. 796 or CourseMate	
	Labs	CourseMate	
Dice	Text	p. 811	Be familiar with Dice's services
	Link	eBook p. 811 or CourseMate	
Dell	Text	p. 811	Be familiar with Dell's products and services
	Link	eBook p. 811 or CourseMate	
Video Resume	Learn How To	pp. 820–821 and CourseMate	Know how to create a video resume
Character Map Utility	Windows Exercises	CourseMate	Know how to use the Character Map Utility
Toggle Keys	Windows Exercises	CourseMate	Know how to use Ease of Access Options to set toggle key actions
Disk Maintenance	Windows Exercises	CourseMate	Know how to use Task Scheduler to schedule disk maintenance
TaxACT Online	Web Apps	CourseMate	Know how to use TaxACT Online to file federal and state taxes

Safe User, Protected from the Risks in a Digital World

Goal: I would like to take measures to (1) protect my computers, devices, and data from loss, damage, or misuse; (2) minimize or prevent risks associated with using technology; and (3) minimize the environmental impact of using computers and related devices.

Topic	Resource	Location	Now you should . . .
Outsourcing	Ethics & Issues	p. 785	Know issues surrounding outsourcing computer jobs
	Video	eBook p. 785 or CourseMate	
Computer Security	FAQ	p. 790	Be familiar with the importance of computer security and ways to secure data and computers
	Link and Video	eBook p. 790 or CourseMate	
Recycling Ink	FAQ	p. 790	Know how to recycle used printer ink cartridges
	FAQ Link	eBook p. 790, or Ink Cartridges link, CourseMate	
Copying Software	Ethics & Issues	p. 791	Know that copying software for purposes other than a backup is illegal

Continued on next page

Continued from previous page

Topic	Resource	Location	Now you should . . .
Personal Information	Ethics & Issues	p. 792	Be aware that IT professionals have access to your personal information
Green Organizations	FAQ	p. 797	Be familiar with strategies organizations use to preserve the environment
	FAQ Link	eBook p. 797, or Green Companies link, CourseMate	

Competent Digital Citizen

Goal: I would like to be knowledgeable and well-informed about computers, mobile devices, and related technology, so that I am digitally literate in my personal and professional use of digital devices.

Topic	Resource	Location	Now you should . . .
Trends	Text/Figure	pp. 784–785	Be familiar with trends related to computer professionals
Generation Gap	Looking Ahead	p. 786	Be familiar with how the generation gap affects IT departments
	Link and Video	eBook p. 786 or CourseMate	
DBA	FAQ	p. 807	Know the difference between database administrator and administration
Computers in Publishing	Computer Usage @ Work	p. 809	Know how authors, writers, and compositors use computers
	Link and Video	eBook p. 809 or CourseMate	
Bioinformatics	Text/Figure	p. 810	Be familiar with informatics and bioinformatics
	Link and Video	eBook p. 810 or CourseMate	
Steve Ballmer	Text	p. 811	Be familiar with Steve Ballmer's contributions to the computer industry
	Link and Video	eBook p. 811 or CourseMate	
Jerry Yang and David Filo	Text	p. 811	Be familiar with Jerry Yang and David Filo's creation
	Link	eBook p. 811 or CourseMate	
Google Tour	Video	At the Movies, CourseMate	Be familiar with Google's facility

Future Entrepreneur or Professional in a Digital Society

Goal: As I ponder my future, I envision myself as an entrepreneur or skilled professional using technology to support my business endeavors or job responsibilities. Along the way, I may interact with a variety of computer professionals — or I may just become one myself!

Topic	Resource	Location	Now you should . . .
IT Department Jobs and Salaries	Text/Figures and FAQ	pp. 786–789	Be familiar with jobs available in an IT department, along with responsibilities and salary ranges
	Drag and Drop Figure 15-3	eBook p. 788-789 or CourseMate	
	FAQ Link	eBook p. 787, or College Graduates' Starting Salaries link, CourseMate	
	Web Link	eBook p. 787 or CourseMate	

Continued on next page

Continued from previous page

Topic	Resource	Location	Now you should . . .
Equipment Field	Text/Figure	p. 790	Be familiar with types of companies and career options in the computer equipment field
Software Field	Text	pp. 790–791	Be familiar with types of companies and career options in the computer software field
Service and Repair Field	Text/Figure and FAQ	pp. 791–792	Be familiar with types of companies and career options in the computer service and repair field
	Figure Video	eBook p. 791 or CourseMate	
	FAQ Link	eBook p. 792, or Diagnostic Tools link, CourseMate	
Sales	Text/Figure	p. 792	Be familiar with types of companies and career options in the computer sales field
Education and Training Field	Text/Figure	pp. 792–793	Be familiar with types of companies and career options in the computer education and training field
IT Consulting	Text and Ethics & Issues	p. 793	Be familiar with career options in the IT consulting field and issues related to consulting mistakes
Career Development	Text/Figures	pp. 797–799	Know ways to keep up to date with industry trends and technologies and to develop new skills: professional organizations and personal networks, professional growth and continuing education, and computer publications and Web sites
	Web Link	eBook p. 797 or CourseMate	
Noncompete Agreements	Ethics & Issues	p. 798	Be aware that some employers require that employees sign a noncompete agreement
Computer Certification	Text/Figures	pp. 800–803	Know the benefits of certification, factors to consider when choosing a certification, how to prepare for certification, and what to expect on the exams
	Link and Video	eBook p. 800 or CourseMate	
	Web Link	eBook p. 801 or CourseMate	
Mainframe Careers	FAQ	p. 802	Know whether a career in mainframes is still a good choice
Application Software Certifications	Text/Figure	p. 804	Be familiar with popular application software certifications, along with careers suited for these certifications
	Web Link	eBook p. 804 or CourseMate	
Operating System Certifications	Text/Figure	p. 804	Be familiar with popular operating system certifications, along with careers suited for these certifications
Programmer/ Developer Certifications	Text/Figure	p. 805	Be familiar with popular programmer/developer certifications, along with careers suited for these certifications
Hardware Certifications	Text/Figure	p. 805	Be familiar with popular hardware certifications, along with careers suited for these certifications
Networking Certifications	Text/Figure	p. 806	Be familiar with popular networking certifications, along with careers suited for these certifications
	Web Link	eBook p. 806	
Digital Forensics Certifications	Text/Figure	p. 806	Be familiar with popular digital forensics certifications, along with careers suited for these certifications
Security Certifications	Text/Figure	p. 807	Be familiar with popular security certifications, along with careers suited for these certifications
Internet Certifications	Text/Figure	p. 807	Be familiar with popular Internet certifications, along with careers suited for these certifications

Continued on next page

Continued from previous page

Topic	Resource	Location	Now you should . . .
Database System Certifications	Text/Figure	pp. 807–808	Be familiar with popular operating system certifications, along with careers suited for these certifications
	FAQ Link	eBook p. 807, or DBA link, CourseMate	
Computer Science/IT Instructor	Exploring Computer Careers	CourseMate	Be familiar with the responsibilities of and education required for a computer science/IT instructor

Preparing for a Test

Visit the Computer Concepts CourseMate at **www.cengagebrain.com** and then navigate to the Chapter 15 Web Apps resource for this book to prepare for your test.

Does your class use the Computer Concepts CourseMate Web site? If so, prepare for your test by using the Flash Cards, Study Guide, and Practice Test Web apps — available for your smart phone or tablet.

If your class does not use the Computer Concepts CourseMate Web site or you prefer to use your book, you can prepare for the test by doing the Quiz Yourself activities on pages 793, 799, and 808; reading the Chapter Review on pages 812–813; ensuring you know the definitions for the terms on page 814; and completing the Checkpoint exercises on pages 815–816. You also should know the material identified in the Chapter 15 Study Guide that follows.

Chapter 15 Study Guide

This study guide identifies material you should know for the Chapter 15 exam. You may want to write the answers in a notebook, enter them on your digital device, record them into a phone, or highlight them in your book. Choose whichever method helps you remember the best.

1. Identify trends with occupations in computer-related fields.

2. Describe issues associated with outsourcing computer jobs.

3. Explain the effect of the generation gap on IT departments.

4. Describe the role of each of these areas in an IT department: management, system development and programming, technical services, operations, training, and security.

5. Identify the function of these IT department jobs: CIO, network administrator, project manager, computer games designer, computer scientist, software engineer, systems analyst, systems programmer, Web software developer, database administrator, digital forensics examiner, graphic designer, Web designer, computer operator, corporate trainer, help desk specialist, CSO, and security administrator.

6. Identify the types of companies involved and career opportunities available in these market segments: computer equipment field, computer software field, computer service and repair field, computer sales, computer education and training field, and IT consulting.

7. Identify recycling programs available for used printer ink cartridges.

8. Describe issues associated with illegal copying of software.

9. Explain how a technician knows how to diagnose a computer problem.

10. Distinguish between trade schools and colleges.

11. Differentiate among various computer-related majors for college students.

12. Identify ways to search for jobs.

13. ACM stands for _____.

14. AITP stands for _____.

15. Define user group.

16. Identify ways to stay current with changing technology after graduation.

17. Identify the purpose of the International Consumer Electronics Show.

18. Identify reasons an employer would want an IT employee to sign a noncompete agreement.

19. Define certification.

20. Explain the role of a sponsoring organization.

21. List the benefits of certification.

22. Identify factors to consider when selecting a certification.

23. Identify ways to prepare for certification.

24. Describe the types of certification exams.

25. List the general areas of IT certification.

26. Describe careers suited for application software certifications. Describe the purpose of these application software certifications: MOS – Core, MOS – Expert, ACE, and ACI.

Continued on next page

Continued from previous page

27. Describe careers suited for operating system certifications. Describe the purpose of these operating system certifications: MCITP, RHCE, and SCSA.

28. Describe careers suited for programmer/developer certifications. Describe the purpose of these programmer/developer certifications: CSDA, IBM Certified Solution Developer, MCPD, and SCMAD.

29. Describe careers suited for hardware certifications. Describe the purpose of this hardware certification: A+.

30. Describe careers suited for networking certifications. Describe the purpose of these networking certifications: NCA, CCNA, Network+, and SCNA.

31. Describe careers suited for digital forensics certifications. Describe the purpose of these digital forensics certifications: CCE and CIFI.

32. Describe careers suited for security certifications. Describe the purpose of these security certifications: CISSP and SCNS.

33. Describe careers suited for Internet certifications. Describe the purpose of this Internet certification: CIW.

34. Describe careers suited for database certifications. Describe the purpose of these database certifications: MCITP and OCP.

35. Define informatics and bioinformatics. Describe the purpose of the Human Genome Project.

36. Describe the purpose of Dice.

37. Identify Steve Ballmer's role with Microsoft.

38. _____ and _____ cofounded Yahoo!.

Check This Out

As technology changes, you must keep up with updates, new products, breakthroughs, and recent advances to remain digitally literate. The list below identifies topics related to this chapter that you should explore to keep current. In parentheses beside each topic, you will find a search term to help begin your research using a search engine, such as Google.

1. new research of how outsourcing actually creates new corporate IT jobs (search for: outsource IT job)
2. recent starting salaries for computer science graduates (search for: starting salary computer science)
3. updates on IT department job functions and salaries (search for: computer job description salary)
4. updates on computer information security jobs (search for: employment computer security)
5. new jobs in the computer equipment field (search for: computer manufacturing distribution jobs)
6. recent computer software career opportunities (search for: software developer manufacture support jobs)
7. popular computer service and repair field jobs (search for: computer service repair jobs)
8. top employment opportunities for computer salespeople (search for: computer sales jobs)
9. current jobs in computer education and training (search for: computer education training jobs)
10. latest IT consulting employment prospects (search for: IT consultant jobs)
11. widely used computer job search techniques and career advice (search for: computer career advice)
12. new recommendations for computer certification training (search for: computer certification)
13. updates about the bioinformatics Human Genome Project (search for: Human Genome Project informatics)
14. latest news about Dell products and company strategies (search for: Dell headlines)
15. popular consumer electronics devices for the home (search for: new consumer electronics home)

For current news and information
Check us out on Facebook and Twitter. See your instructor or the Computer Concepts CourseMate for specific information.

Quick Reference

Quick Reference

Every chapter in this Student Success Guide presents tables of resources targeted toward one of five student goals: informed digital consumer; productive technology user; safe user, protected from the risks in a digital world; competent digital citizen; and future entrepreneur or professional in a digital society. Resources may be located in the textbook, on the Computer Concepts CourseMate Web site, in the Interactive eBook, and on the Web.

Some of the tables throughout the Student Success Guide identify text and/or a figure(s) as the resource, which you will find self-explanatory. For those resources that are not identified as text or figures, the following table provides a quick reference to help you locate each type of resource. The first and second columns name and briefly describe the resource and its purpose. The third column identifies where you can find the resource and, in brackets, outlines how to navigate to resources on the Computer Concepts CourseMate Web site (www.cengagebrain.com). For more detailed instructions about the Computer Concepts CourseMate, refer to the pages specified in the fourth column.

Resource	Purpose	Location [Navigation]	Additional Information
Animations	Strengthen your understanding of chapter topics through animations that correspond directly to book content	Interactive eBook	• 1 per chapter
			For further instruction, see page 97 in CourseMate Student Guide
		CourseMate [eBook Interactive Activities link on navigation menu | Animations tab]	For further instruction, see page 97 in CourseMate Student Guide
Companies on the Cutting Edge	Expose you to companies you should know in the computer industry	Last page in chapter before Student Assignments	• 2 per chapter
		CourseMate [Beyond the Book link on navigation menu | Beyond the Book tab]	For further instruction, see page 104 in CourseMate Student Guide
Computer Usage @ Work	Familiarize you with ways various industries use computers and related technology	Follows Chapter Summary	• 1 per chapter
		External links with more information on **CourseMate** [Beyond the Book link on navigation menu | Beyond the Book tab]	For further instruction, see page 104 in CourseMate Student Guide
Drag and Drop Figures	Boost your understanding of chapter visuals through interactive figure activities	Interactive eBook	For further instruction, see page 97 in CourseMate Student Guide
		CourseMate [eBook Interactive Activities link on navigation menu | Drag and Drop Figures tab]	For further instruction, see page 97 in CourseMate Student Guide
Ethics & Issues	Heighten your awareness of ethical and controversial computer-related issues	Boxes throughout textbook	• 4 to 5 per chapter • For complete list of topics, see page xii in textbook
		CourseMate [Beyond the Book link on navigation menu | Ethics & Issues tab]	For further instruction, see page 104 in CourseMate Student Guide
Exploring Computer Careers	Familiarize you with various professions in the computer industry	**CourseMate** [Activities and Tutorials link on navigation menu | Exploring Computer Careers tab]	For further instruction, see page 97 in CourseMate Student Guide
FAQs	Ask and answer intriguing or current event questions related to technology	Boxes throughout textbook	• 6 to 8 per chapter • For complete list of topics, see pages xii-xiii in textbook
		External links with more information on **CourseMate** [Beyond the Book link on navigation menu | Beyond the Book tab]	For further instruction, see page 104 in CourseMate Student Guide

Continued on next page

Continued from previous page

High-Tech Talk	Deepen your knowledge of computer-related topics through technical discussions	Page following Chapter Summary	• 1 per chapter
		External links with more information on **CourseMate** [Beyond the Book link on navigation menu | Beyond the Book tab]	For further instruction, see page 104 in CourseMate Student Guide
Innovative Computing	Explore original or creative uses of technology to solve traditional problems	Boxes throughout textbook	• 1 to 2 per chapter • For complete list of topics, see page xiii in textbook
		External links with more information on **CourseMate** [Beyond the Book link on navigation menu | Beyond the Book tab]	For further instruction, see page 104 in CourseMate Student Guide
Labs (Student Edition Labs)	Reinforce and expand your knowledge about basic computer topics	**CourseMate** [Student Edition Labs link on navigation menu]	For further instruction, see page 100 in CourseMate Student Guide
Learn How To	Learn fundamental technology skills for practical everyday tasks through hands-on activities and exercises	Student Assignments in textbook	• 1 to 3 per chapter
		CourseMate [Video Study Tools link on navigation menu | Learn How To tab]	For further instruction, see page 103 in CourseMate Student Guide
Looking Ahead	Alert you to upcoming technological breakthroughs or recent advances in the industry	Boxes throughout textbook	• 1 per chapter • For complete list of topics, see page xiii in textbook
		External links with more information on **CourseMate** [Beyond the Book link on navigation menu | Beyond the Book tab]	For further instruction, see page 104 in CourseMate Student Guide
Technology Trailblazers	Expose you to leaders you should know in the computer industry	Last page in chapter before Student Assignments	• 2 per chapter
		CourseMate [Beyond the Book link on navigation menu | Beyond the Book tab]	For further instruction, see page 104 in CourseMate Student Guide
Videos	Show you current information or varying perspectives through third-party videos	Interactive eBook	For further instruction, see page 97 in CourseMate Student Guide
		CourseMate [eBook Interactive Activities link on navigation menu | Videos tab]	For further instruction, see page 97 in CourseMate Student Guide
		CourseMate [Video Study Tools link on navigation menu | At the Movies tab]	For further instruction, see page 103 in CourseMate Student Guide
Web Apps	Learn how to use popular Web apps through practical exercises	**CourseMate** [Activities and Tutorials link on navigation menu | Web Apps tab]	For further instruction, see page 97 in CourseMate Student Guide
Web Links	Present you with current information or varying perspectives through external Web sites	**CourseMate** [Beyond the Book link on navigation menu | Beyond the Book tab]	For further instruction, see page 104 in CourseMate Student Guide
Windows Exercises	Sharpen your Windows skills by stepping through exercises on your computer	**CourseMate** [Activities and Tutorials link on navigation menu | Activities and Tutorials tab]	For further instruction, see page 100 in CourseMate Student Guide

Computer Concepts
CourseMate
Student Guide

Computer Concepts CourseMate Student Guide

Introduction

Welcome to this Computer Concepts CourseMate Student Guide. Computer Concepts CourseMate is an online collection of tools and resources you can use to enrich the learning process with the *Discovering Computers: Your Interactive Guide to the Digital World* textbook. This guide will help familiarize you with the navigation of the tools and resources contained in Computer Concepts CourseMate.

To use Computer Concepts CourseMate while following along in this guide, you will need access to:

- A computer
- An Internet connection
- A Web browser

Getting Started on Computer Concepts CourseMate

Computer Concepts CourseMate, which is a Web-based companion to the *Discovering Computers* textbook, is an easy-to-use and innovative product designed to enhance your learning experience. Access Computer Concepts CourseMate by navigating to http://login.cengagebrain.com in a Web browser. Set up a user name if you do not have one already, log in, and then use the printed access code to register your Computer Concepts CourseMate product.

After successful login to Computer Concepts CourseMate, the My Dashboard page will be displayed (Figure 1). On the My Dashboard page, follow these steps to add the *Discovering Computers* textbook to your bookshelf:

1. Type the title ISBN, author name, or title in the 'Add a title to your bookshelf' text box.
2. Click the Search button to display the Discovering Computers product on your bookshelf.

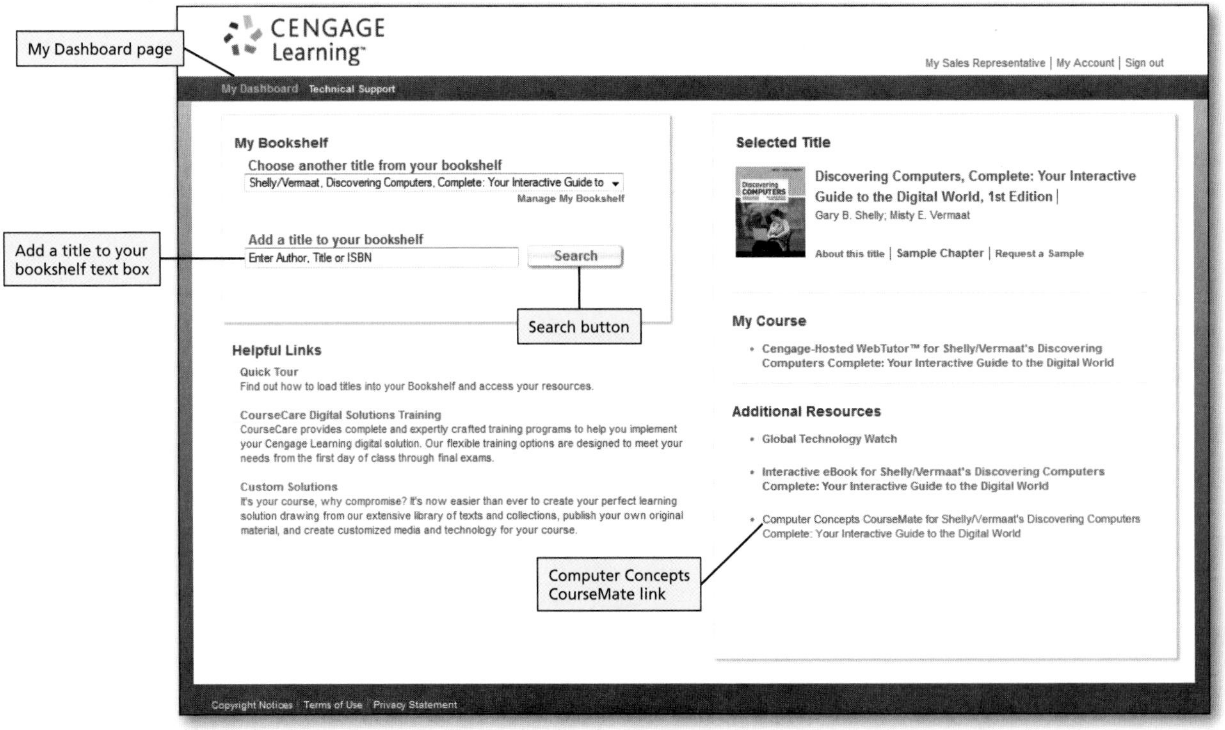

Figure 1

Once the book is added to your bookshelf, its associated Computer Concepts CourseMate link will be listed in the Additional Resources area of this page (shown in Figure 1). Click the Computer Concepts CourseMate link, which in this case, is called Computer Concepts CourseMate for Shelly/Vermaat's Discovering Computers Complete: Your Interactive Guide to the Digital World, to open the Computer Concepts CourseMate for *Discovering Computers* (Figure 2).

Figure 2

Using the Interactive eBook

You can access all of the textbook content through Computer Concepts CourseMate's Interactive eBook on your desktop or mobile computer, as long as you have an Internet connection. Open the Interactive eBook by clicking the Chapter eBook link on the navigation menu (shown in Figure 2), which is located on the left side of Computer Concepts CourseMate. The Interactive eBook not only displays all of the information in the text but also includes many interactive tools that are not available in the printed textbook. Figure 3 on the next page identifies specific tools in the Interactive eBook. For a brief description about how to use each of the tools, click the Help button in the upper-right corner of the Interactive eBook.

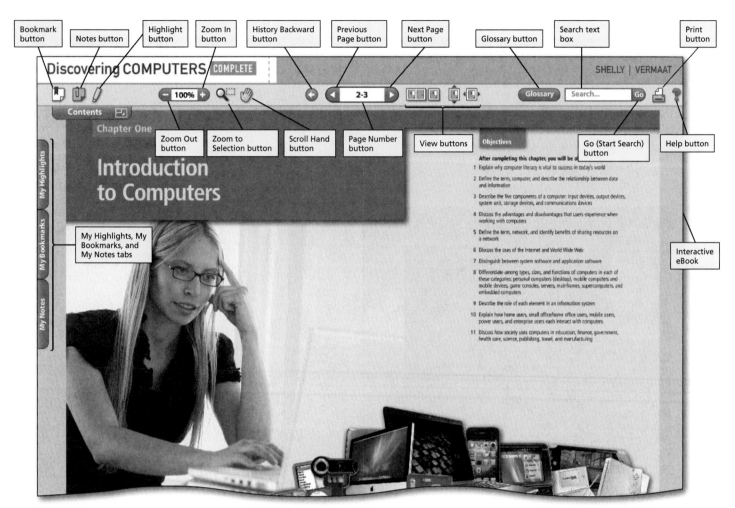

Figure 3

You can browse quickly through pages of text in the Interactive eBook, search for a term, zoom in to a section of a page, view multiple page layouts, take notes on a specific item, highlight text, bookmark a section, or search the glossary for a specific key term by using the buttons identified in Figure 3. To display all of your highlights, bookmarks, or notes, click the respective tabs on the left side of the Interactive eBook; or, you can print your highlights or notes using the Print button in the upper-right corner of the Interactive eBook. To display a different chapter or feature, click the Table of Contents button in the upper-left corner and then click the desired chapter on the menu.

Key terms, which are shaded gray throughout the Interactive eBook for easy identification, are links. Click any key term to display the Mini Glossary, where you can view the definition of the key term, listen to an audio recording of the term, and display external links associated with the term (Figure 4).

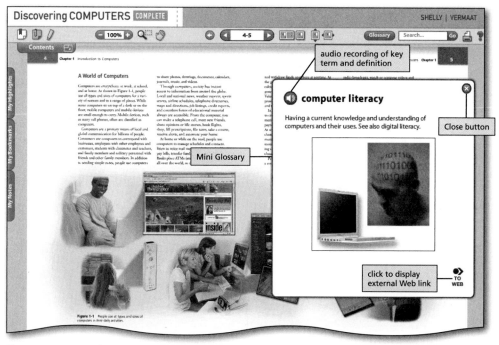

Figure 4

Learning Key Terms and Definitions

Computer Concepts CourseMate includes multiple resources to help you learn the terms and concepts in the *Discovering Computers* textbook. These resources include Interactive Flashcards, Key Terms, and games.

Instead of using index cards to create your own flashcards, you can use the Interactive Flashcards in Computer Concepts CourseMate to learn, review, and test your knowledge of key terms (Figure 5). These flashcards appear on the screen and look similar to those you would make yourself. While using the Interactive Flashcards, you can choose to display the definition or the term first, shuffle the deck, remove terms, or show all cards. If you simply want a list of the glossary items in one place for quick reference, click the Key Terms link, instead of the Interactive Flashcards link, on the navigation menu on the left side of Computer Concepts CourseMate.

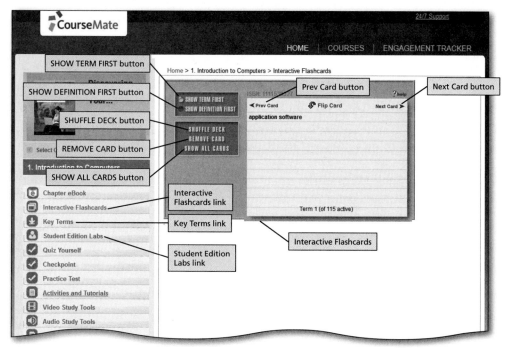

Figure 5

Do you want to challenge your knowledge of chapter content? The Crossword Puzzle resource covers the chapter's key terms and definitions. The Crossword Puzzle is a timed activity, which provides options to check your answers, undo incorrect answers, and submit your final solution. Complete the crossword puzzle to solidify your knowledge of the key terms and their definitions. To access the Crossword Puzzle resource, click the Activities and Tutorials link on the navigation menu on the left side of Computer Concepts CourseMate.

Wheel of Terms is another fun Computer Concepts CourseMate learning tool that tests your key term knowledge (Figure 6). Spin the wheel, pick a letter, buy a vowel, or submit your answer to the definition shown above the board. As you solve the puzzle and earn game money, you also build confidence for an upcoming exam. To access the Wheel of Terms resource, click the Activities and Tutorials link on the navigation menu on the left side of Computer Concepts CourseMate.

Figure 6

Hands-On Labs and Exercises

Computer Concepts CourseMate includes a variety of hands-on resources so that you can practice items covered in the textbook. Two of these resources are the Student Edition Labs and Windows Exercises.

To display the Student Edition Labs associated with a chapter, click the Student Edition Labs link on the navigation menu, which is located on the left side of Computer Concepts CourseMate (shown in Figure 5 on the previous page). You can start any individual lab in the list by clicking its link and then clicking the Start button for the lab. Figure 7 shows a sample lab and identifies elements of the interface.

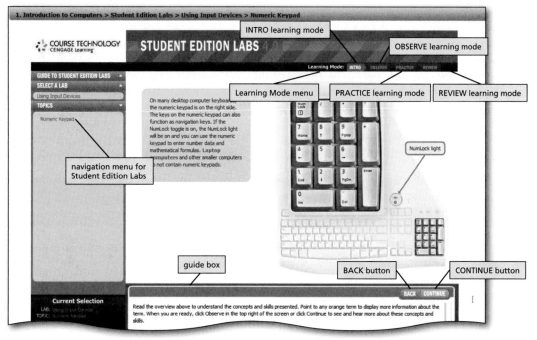

Figure 7

You interact with labs through four learning modes: Intro, Observe, Practice, and Review (shown in Figure 7). Each mode is designed to provide a cohesive path to learning the task. The Intro learning mode presents an overview of the topic; the Observe learning mode provides audio and visual guides; the Practice learning mode offers step-by-step instructions; and the Review learning mode supplies a series of multiple choice questions. At the bottom of each learning mode screen is a guide box that contains instructions for completing the lab and buttons for navigating through the lab.

Each Computer Concepts CourseMate chapter offers several Windows Exercises tailored to accompany the textbook and expand your knowledge of Windows. These step-by-step exercises vary by chapter and should be performed on a local computer. To access the Windows Exercises, click the Activities and Tutorials link on the navigation menu on the left side of the Computer Concepts CourseMate and then click the desired Windows Exercise.

Comprehensive Test Preparation

Computer Concepts CourseMate not only supplies resources to help you learn the chapter content, it also can help prepare you for quizzes and tests. Gauge your knowledge before a chapter exam using these resources: Computer Genius, Quiz Yourself, Checkpoint, You're Hired!, and Practice Test.

Who wants to be a Computer Genius? Are you ready to test your knowledge? Computer Genius tests your knowledge of the chapter content in a game-show environment. Start the Computer Genius game by clicking the Activities and Tutorials link on the Computer Concepts CourseMate navigation menu and then clicking the Computer Genius link. Computer Genius is a timed, multiple choice quiz that will test your knowledge of important concepts, terms, and ideas in the chapter text. If you are stumped on a question, use the Panic Buttons, such as the Book, 50/50, Survey, Double-Dip, and 3 Professors, before submitting your final answer.

Are you ready to look for a job? The You're Hired! game tests your understanding of chapter key terms in an interactive, timed simulation. In this simulation, you answer questions based on chapter content at a career fair, in an internship, and then in a job interview, to prove you are the right person for the job. If you answer questions incorrectly, the You're Hired! game allows you to repeat the level or to print a study guide to refine your answers for the time you play. To access You're Hired!, click the Activities and Tutorials link on the Computer Concepts CourseMate navigation menu and then click the You're Hired! link.

Prepare for your next quiz using the Quiz Yourself resource. The quizzes are grouped by chapter objectives. To begin a quiz, click the Quiz Yourself link on the Computer Concepts CourseMate navigation menu, click the desired objective groups on the Objectives tabs at the top of the screen, read the instructions, and then click the Start button. When you are finished taking the quiz, click the Done button and review your score and results. Results on the Quiz Summary screen are cross-referenced with the textbook and the Interactive eBook. If you have an incorrect answer, you can click the magnifying glass icon to the right of the answer to display the location of the correct answer in the textbook and the Interactive eBook (Figure 8).

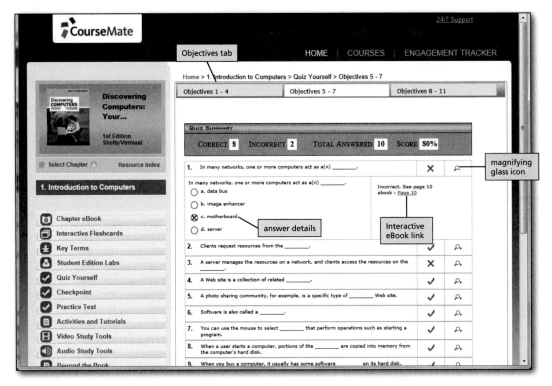

Figure 8

The Checkpoint resource checks your key term and chapter knowledge using matching, true/false, and multiple choice questions. When you click the Checkpoint link on the Computer Concepts CourseMate navigation menu, the first screen displays the Matching activity; to switch to True/False or Multiple Choice, click the desired name on the Checkpoint tabs at the top of the screen. Begin any of the activities by clicking the Start button. When you are finished with the activity, click the Done button, and review your results. Like the Quiz Yourself activity, you can cross-reference your responses using the magnifying glass icon.

The Practice Test is the most comprehensive tool to test your chapter knowledge (Figure 9). Because the Practice Test simulates a real test, it is an extremely important resource on Computer Concepts CourseMate. Click the Practice Test link on the Computer Concepts CourseMate navigation menu to begin the test. As with the other quizzes on Computer Concepts CourseMate, all answers are verified and your score appears after you click the Done button. All answers include a magnifying glass icon, which, when clicked, provides a cross-reference to the textbook and the Interactive eBook. In preparation for the best results on the real exam, try to achieve a 100 percent score on the Practice Test.

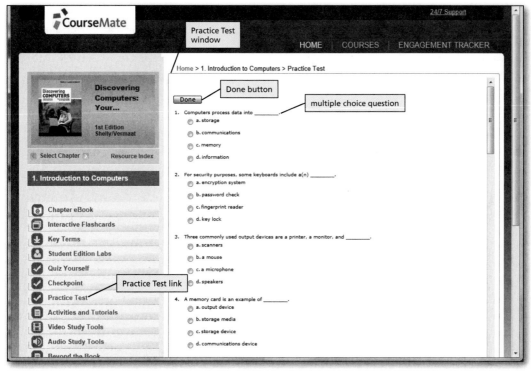

Figure 9

Enhanced Study Aids

Computer Concepts CourseMate includes both audio and video tools to further enhance your learning experience with the *Discovering Computers* textbook. The Video Study Tools, accessed from the Computer Concepts CourseMate navigation menu by clicking the Video Study Tools link, include these tools: You Review It, At the Movies, Learn How To, and Quiz: Learn How To. To use a particular tool, click its name on the Video Study Tools tabs at the top of the screen. The first three tools use videos, podcasts, or vodcasts of content related to the textbook; the Learn How To Quiz tests your knowledge of the material in the Learn How To video resource.

Sometimes, if you listen to text being read, you might absorb it into memory better than if you read it. For this reason, Computer Concepts CourseMate provides audio files of key terms and chapter content. To access these audio files, click the Audio Study Tools link on the Computer Concepts CourseMate navigation menu (Figure 10 on the next page). Audio tools are available for both the Chapter Review and the chapter key terms. Access each by clicking the respective resource name on the Audio Study Tools tabs at the top of the screen. Read the on-screen instructions, then download the audio files to a local computer or preferred portable media player, so that you can listen to the audio files offline.

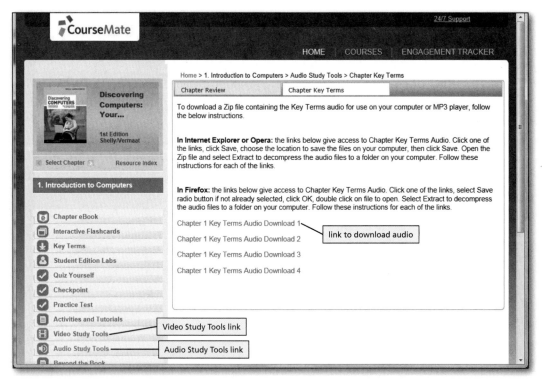

Figure 10

Explore Other Resources

Your *Discovering Computers* textbook presents a great wealth of information; Computer Concepts CourseMate expands on this information with the Beyond the Book and Ethics & Issues resources. Click the Beyond the Book link on the Computer Concepts CourseMate navigation menu to display a host of external links that are referenced throughout the chapter text. Click any link to explore resources outside of the Computer Concepts CourseMate interface. If you click Ethics & Issues on the Beyond the Book tabs at the top of the screen, text from all of the Ethics & Issues boxes in the chapter will be displayed in one convenient location. Learn, explore, and provide answers to various ethical questions pertaining to chapter topics.

Book-Level Resources at the bottom of the Computer Concepts CourseMate navigation menu include the following: Install Computer, Maintain Computer, Timeline, Buyer's Guide, Digital Forensics, Making Use of the Web, and Global Technology Watch (Figure 11). Each of these tools is designed to enhance your *Discovering Computers* experience by providing additional information or external, third-party links.

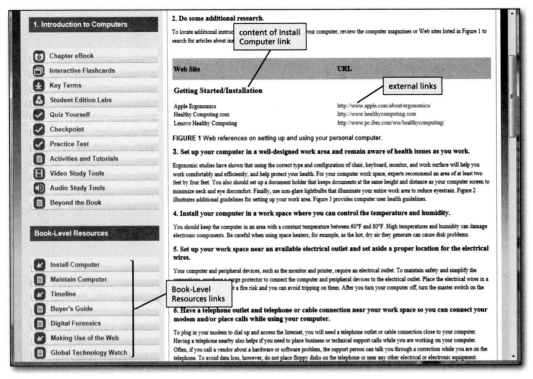

Figure 11

New Web Apps

New to Computer Concepts CourseMate for *Discovering Computers* are three Web applications (Web apps) that aid student comprehension of chapter material. These Web apps are available only via Computer Concepts CourseMate and are developed for use on smart phones, as well as on tablets, notebook computers, and desktop computers.

Improve retention of the chapter key terms with the Flashcard Web app. Study for an exam by reviewing major points in each chapter with the Study Guide Web app or with the Practice Test Web app that provides multiple choice questions.

Use the new Web apps as part of your overall *Discovering Computers* learning experience to help you succeed using *Discovering Computers*.

Summary

Computer Concepts CourseMate is designed for use as a companion to the *Discovering Computers: Your Interactive Guide to the Digital World* textbook. Conveniently organized in one location, all of the tools and resources in Computer Concepts CourseMate will help you learn. You can leave your book at home and use the Interactive eBook, study key terms, work on a simulated lab or explore other activities, download audio of key terms, watch a video related to the chapter text, take a practice quiz or exam, extend your learning experience outside of the book with external resources, and much more! Computer Concepts CourseMate is designed carefully to help you succeed using *Discovering Computers*.

WebTutor
Student Guide

WebTutor Student Guide

Objectives

You will have mastered the material in this guide when you can:

- Log in to Angel and Blackboard to access WebTutor content
- View Topic Reviews, PowerPoint Presentations, Practice Tests, and Topic Review Questions in Course Documents
- View Assignments
- Access and complete Assessments and Activities

Introduction

Welcome to the Discovering Computers 2012 Student Guide to WebTutor. The purpose of this guide is to orient you to the WebTutor online tools, which supplement the *Discovering Computers: Your Interactive Guide to the Digital World* textbooks. The WebTutor online materials will assist you with interactive ways of learning the material in your textbook.

Log in to Angel or Blackboard

You can access WebTutor via the Web applications Angel or Blackboard. In this section, you will log in to each of these applications.

Access WebTutor in Angel

Log in to Angel The following steps log in to Angel to access WebTutor.

- Start a Web browser, navigate to your school's Angel site, and then log in.
- Click the appropriate Discovering Computers ©2012 title in the Courses list to display information for the course in which you are enrolled (Figure 1).

Figure 1

Access WebTutor in Blackboard

Log in to Blackboard The following steps log in to Blackboard to access WebTutor.

- Start a Web browser, navigate to your school's Blackboard site, and then log in.

- Click the Courses tab, if necessary, to view the course list.

- Click the appropriate Discovering Computers ©2012 title in the course list to display information for the course in which you are enrolled (Figure 2).

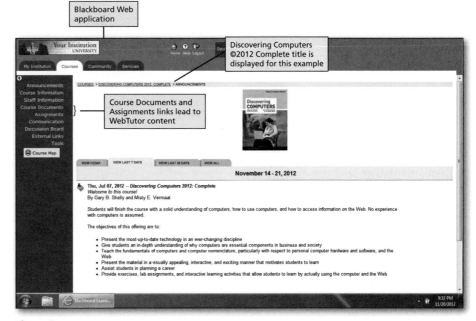

Figure 2

Course Documents

WebTutor contains course documents that reinforce the textbook content. The types of course documents are Topic Review, PowerPoint Presentations, Practice Test, and Topic Review Questions. In order to access course documents, log in to a WebTutor application (Angel or Blackboard) and then navigate to the course documents. Within the course documents are links to each chapter of the textbook. Click a chapter's link to display the list of WebTutor course documents for that chapter.

Topic Review

The WebTutor Topic Review is a course document that corresponds to the textbook's Chapter Review, which is located in the Student Assignments section of each chapter. Figure 3 shows a sample WebTutor Topic Review course document in Angel and Blackboard. Each link in the Topic Review corresponds to one of the statements or questions in bold in the textbook's Chapter Review. After thinking about the instruction and your response, click the corresponding link to view the answer, which also is located in the Chapter Review in the textbook. Table 1 shows the click path to the WebTutor Topic Review in each application.

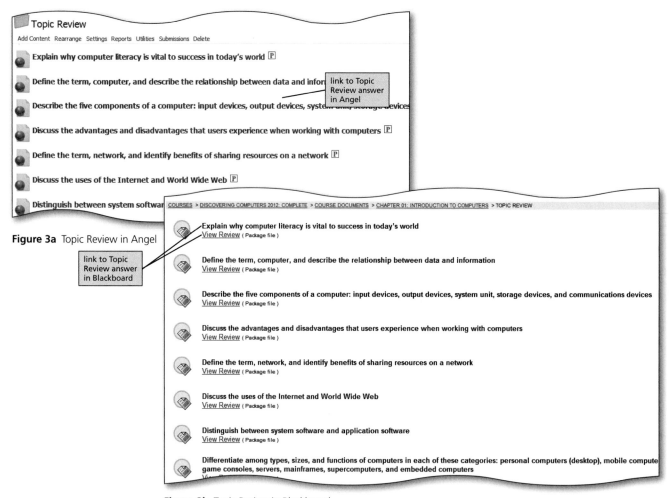

Figure 3a Topic Review in Angel

Figure 3b Topic Review in Blackboard

Figure 3

Table 1 Topic Review Click Path (substitute the chapter number in place of the * in the path)	
WEB APPLICATION	PATH
Angel	Lessons tab > Course Documents > Chapter * > Topic Review
Blackboard	Courses tab > Course Documents > Chapter * > Topic Review

PowerPoint Presentations

WebTutor contains PowerPoint presentations to reinforce the textbook content. Each PowerPoint presentation shows a high-level overview of the textbook chapter's contents. The presentations begin with the same image contained on the textbook chapter's first page, and the slides highlight key terms and figures in the chapter. The slides also contain graphical representations of lists of important information to remember. For example, Figure 4 shows slides from the presentation for Chapter 1 of the Discovering Computers 2012 Complete textbook. On the PowerPoint Presentations in each WebTutor application, you either can view a presentation online in a browser or download the presentation. Table 2 shows the click path to the WebTutor PowerPoint Presentations in each application.

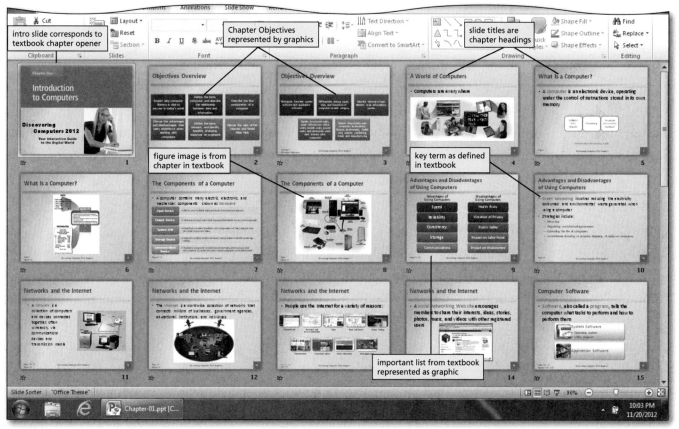

Figure 4

Table 2 PowerPoint Presentations Click Path (substitute the chapter number in place of the * in the path)	
WEB APPLICATION	PATH
Angel	Lessons tab > Course Documents > Chapter * > PowerPoint Presentations
Blackboard	Courses tab > Course Documents > Chapter * > PowerPoint Presentations

Practice Test

The WebTutor Practice Test is a course document that presents an extensive online test, which you can use to practice answering questions about the material covered in a chapter (Figure 5). Because the Practice Test is not printed in the textbook, you will find this tool useful in studying for your exams. The content for the questions is taken from the textbook and will reinforce the information. Also, practicing answering the questions will help prepare you for answering exam questions.

When you have completed a Practice Test, you can submit it for a grade. If desired, you can retake the test to improve your grade; only the latest grade is recorded in the online grade book. The test likely will include multiple choice, true/false, completion, matching, and/or essay questions. Table 3 shows the click path to the WebTutor Practice Test in each application.

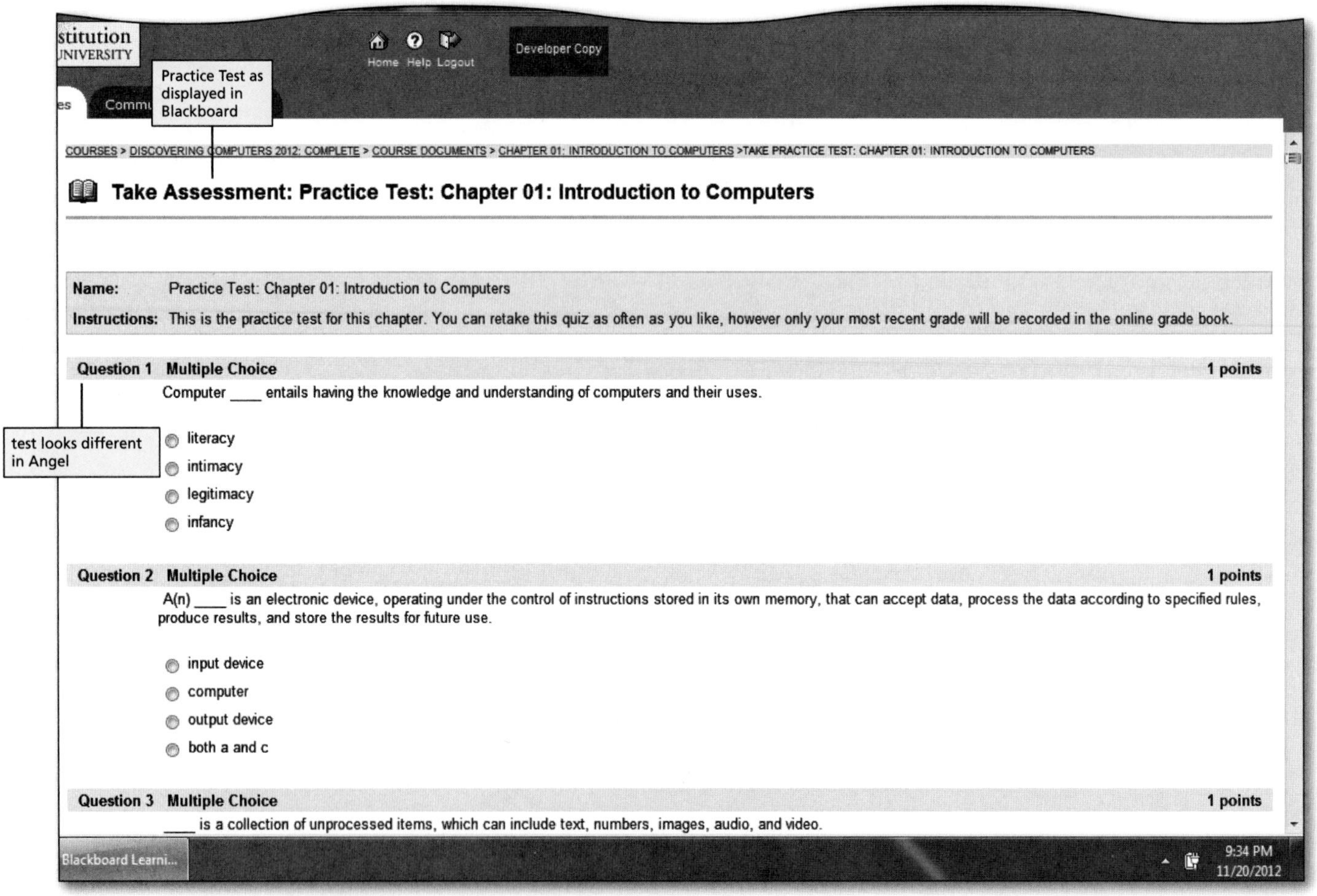

Figure 5

Table 3 Practice Test Click Path (substitute the chapter number in place of the * in the path)	
WEB APPLICATION	PATH
Angel	Lessons tab > Quizzes > Practice Test: Chapter *
	Lessons tab > Question Banks > Practice Test: Chapter *
Blackboard	Courses tab > Course Documents > Chapter * > Practice Test

Topic Review Questions

The Topic Review Questions are an abbreviated version of the Practice Tests that you can use to practice answering possible test questions about the material covered in the chapter (Figure 6). Like the Practice Test, the Topic Review Questions are not located in the textbook. Topic Review Questions can be used as a quick self-assessment tool to gauge how well you know the textbook chapter's material. As with the Practice Test, practicing answering the questions will help prepare you for answering exam questions.

After completing the quiz, you can submit it for a grade. If desired, you can retake the quiz to improve your grade; only the latest grade is recorded in the online grade book. This short quiz could include true/false, multiple choice, and completion questions. Table 4 shows the click path to the WebTutor Topic Review Questions in each application.

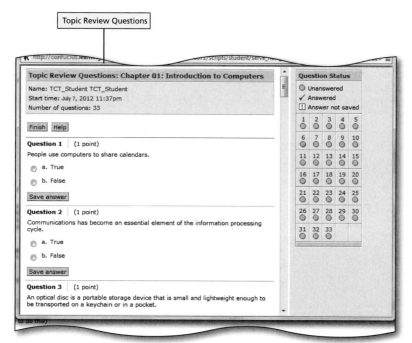

Figure 6

Table 4 Topic Review Questions Click Path (substitute the chapter number in place of the * in the path)	
WEB APPLICATION	PATH
Angel	Lessons tab > Quizzes > Topic Review Questions: Chapter *
	Lessons tab > Question Banks > Topic Review Questions: Chapter *
Blackboard	Courses tab > Course Documents > Chapter * > Topic Review Questions

Assignments

Assignments in WebTutor are additional materials designed to enhance your understanding of the information in the textbook. The content of the assignments varies by title and chapter and includes an assignment topic that links to a suggested exercise (Figure 7a). When you click a link, the suggested exercise will appear (Figure 7b). Your instructor may assign the essay to you, or you may choose to complete an assignment to better understand topics in the textbook. Table 5 shows the click path to the WebTutor Assignments in each application.

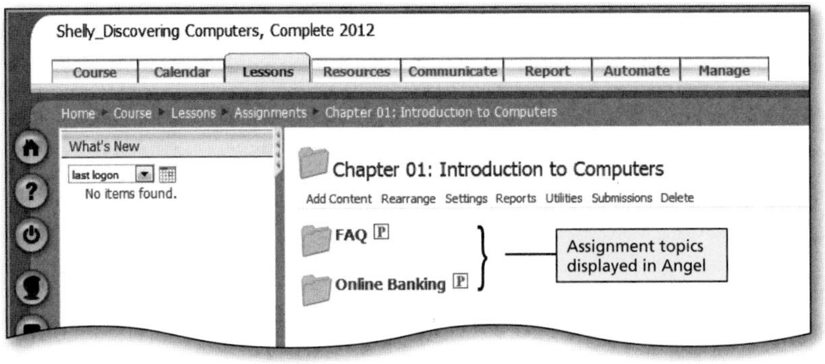

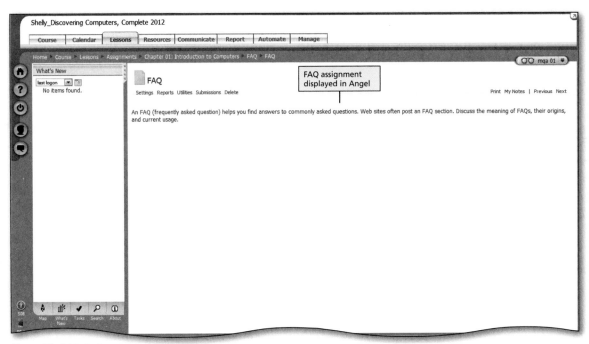

Figure 7a Assignment Topics

Figure 7b FAQ Assignment

Figure 7

Table 5 Assignments Click Path	
(substitute the chapter number in place of the * in the path)	
WEB APPLICATION	PATH
Angel	Lessons tab > Assignments > Chapter *
Blackboard	Courses tab > Assignments > Chapter *

Summary

The WebTutor online course documents — Topic Reviews, PowerPoint Presentations, Practice Tests, and Topic Review Questions, and Assignments — reinforce the information in the Discovering Computers ©2012 textbooks. You can access the WebTutor online tools using the Angel or Blackboard Web applications.